PRAISE

When Heaven Hits Home

Myles and Katharine are Messianic leaders with a balanced theology who offer practical tools for living a joyful faith-filled life. Their sense of humor and chemistry come through in this book and I am glad to count them as friends on the journey to Messiah's return.

Rabbi Jonathan Bernis, President,
Jewish Voice Ministries International

I am honored to travel the world. One of the most delightful couples I have ever met through all of my journeys and connections is Myles and Katharine Weiss. Their marriage represents what God is doing on the earth—"One New Man." More importantly, they represent unity, alignment, and working together. You will be blessed by reading their book since not only will you get to know them, but you will also learn what it means to come into a true blood-covenant relationship with the Lord. This is a season when Heaven and Earth are aligning, and you are key in that alignment. When Heaven Hits Home will help you understand how Heaven and Earth can be aligned through people like yourself. Don't miss the joy you will receive by entering in!

Dr. Chuck D. Pierce, President,
Global Spheres, Inc.; President,
Glory of Zion International Ministries

Myles and Katharine Weiss' wonderful book When Heaven Hits Home: Ancient Wisdom for Today's Couples *is a unique treasury of wisdom and insights, gleaned from their decades of experience in family counseling, as well as walking out their own personal challenges of a Jewish-Gentile "one new man" relationship. Infused with Myles' hilarious descriptions, and incorporating the beauty and richness of biblical Jewish roots, this book is truly a gift to the Body of Messiah.* When Heaven Hits Home *will definitely be my first choice of recommended books for couples at any season of married life.*

> **Karen Davis**, Worship Director/
> Recording Artist, Carmel Congregation,
> Haifa, Israel

Myles and Katharine Weiss weave together their own remarkable story with practical and sound counsel for married couples—and all prescribed with a heaping spoonful of good humor. I read it all in one sitting. You'll love it, too. And make sure you try this at home!

> **Wayne Hilsden**, Cofounder,
> King of Kings Community, Jerusalem;
> President, Fellowship of Israel Related
> Ministries (FIRM)

A beautiful book, simple to read and inspiring toward marriage renewal and success.

> **Dr. Daniel C. Juster**, Founder and Director,
> Tikkun International

Enjoyed the read. When Heaven Hits Home *draws you in quickly. It's an intriguing read, delving into the Hebrew to reveal the gift of marriage. This book is a beautiful love story of two different people coming from two different lifestyles, championing the importance of keeping God as the center in their marriage.*

Beni Johnson, Bethel Church,
Redding, CA; Author,
Happy Intercessor and *Healthy & Free*

I love everything about this book! I have learned so much from Myles and Katharine through the years and I rejoice that their unique love story, peppered with humor and solid relationship insights, has finally made it to print. You'll enjoy every page!

Dr. Ed Silvoso, Founder & President,
Harvest Evangelism and Transform Our
World Network; Author,
*Ekklesia: Rediscovering God's Instrument
for Global Transformation*

How many opportunities are there to gain insights into building a successful marriage relationship from a Messianic Jew who is ALSO a marriage counselor? I highly recommend this book! It is insightful, thought provoking, and fun to read.

Rabbi Kirt A. Schneider, Evangelist and
Host, *Discovering the Jewish Jesus*

When Heaven Hits Home

When Heaven Hits Home

Ancient Wisdom
for Today's Couples

Katharine and Myles Weiss, MA, MFT

With a Foreword by Dr. James Garlow, Ph.D.,
and
Rosemary Schindler-Garlow

WHEN HEAVEN HITS HOME:
Ancient Wisdom for Today's Couples

by Katharine and Myles Weiss, MA, MFT

Copyright 2018 Katharine and Myles Weiss

ISBN: 978-1-7328632-0-0

Editing Consultant: Michelle Shelfer, benediction.biz
Layout and Interior Design: Janet Long

Printed by Color House Graphics in the United States of America.

DEDICATION

To Messiah Yeshua, Who gives our life
meaning and purpose.

To our two wonderful sons, Jonathan and Stephen.

To our daughter-in-love, Rebecca Lamb Weiss.

To David Davis, of blessed memory,
whose message changed the course of our lives.

TABLE OF CONTENTS

FOREWORD

Myles and Katharine have walked the path of reconciliation for many years. It begins with their marriage and in their home. They are profoundly different from each other, but they have allowed the Spirit to shape them into a beautiful picture of God's love. We have worked together with them to see Jews, Christians, and the nations find commonality and love. I rejoiced at the insight, humor, and accessibility of their story.

This book reveals the seamless connection between the Hebrew Scriptures and the New Testament, with practical applications for everyday life. The background for the book is the mystery of the rebirth of Israel and the awakening of faith in God's chosen people. You will find ancient wisdom for modern life, expressed with a poignancy developed through thirty years of ministry together. The writing is insightful, brisk, succinct, engaging, compelling, and just plain fun.

In our day, as so many marriages struggle to survive, it is refreshing to realize that the God of Abraham provides practical tools so our marriages can thrive. The cosmic love story of redemption through the Messiah of Israel is prophetically pictured in the sacred commitment of man and woman.

We heartily recommend this book to all who are seeking a deeper, more joyful understanding of God's abundant life.

Dr. James Garlow, Ph.D.
Pastor Emeritus,
Skyline Church, San Diego, CA

Rosemary Schindler-Garlow,
President,
Schindler's Ark

ACKNOWLEDGMENTS

We are grateful to the many mentors and friends who have touched our lives. Our parents, Ed and Janis Burke, and Paul and Hannah Weiss, set a standard of working it out rather than giving it up.

Dr. Mitch Glaser and his team convinced me I was not the first Jewish person to fall in love with Jesus as Messiah.

The Azusa Pacific faculty and Bethel Church helped form our perspectives on different aspects of healing.

Rosemary Schindler-Garlow encouraged us to pursue the shared destiny of Israel and the community of faith.

The Mount Carmel team revolutionized our ministry.

Chuck Pierce believed in Israel's significance and our role in helping the church know it.

The Father's House made room for our call.

Beth Shalom/House of Peace believed that this message should go "from Golden Gate to Golden Gate."

Zola Levitt Presents confirmed our desire to touch the entire world with the message of God's reconciliation.

Our friends in Israel and around the world provided wisdom and a doctrinal safety net.

Michelle Shelfer edited this work with professional vigor and served alongside us in love.

Over the years, our dear friend Cheryl Geyer became our trusted assistant, heroically going the extra mile.

To all these, we say a hearty *todah rabah*, or thank you!

INTRODUCTION

Call me Mordechai, which is my given Hebrew name. Pastors call me Rabbi. Rabbis say Pastor. Counselees say Doc. My New York family calls me *meshugah*, which is Yiddish for "crazy," because I am a Jewish follower of Yeshua (Jesus). God called me to Himself in 1984. For years I wandered through a hippie paradigm of New Age philosophies and excruciating darkness. A light that was brighter than any star beckoned when I was thirty-three years old. I was irresistibly drawn to the "luminous figure of the Nazarene," as Albert Einstein described Jesus.[1]

This epiphany did not instantaneously alleviate all the human need in me or around me. Suffering still seems to be a major part of our learning curve in this life. However, my journey began with high adventure that has allowed me to peer into the hearts of people. I have watched in awe as the scarred hands of Yeshua, the wounded healer, touched them. May that same healing touch reach from these pages into your heart.

We've all heard Cinderella stories about the unlikely young man or woman from humble origins who manages to marry up, snagging a handsome prince or beautiful princess who is way beyond their social standing or economic status. Truth be told, that is the story of Katharine and me as well! Anyone who follows the Messiah of the world has experienced just that sort of elevation in a different kind of bride/bridegroom relationship, that communion between Yeshua and His "called-out ones" (Jesus and His Church). We are lifted out of our earthbound lives into an eternal and perfect heavenly marriage. Just as the relationship between Jesus and His Church is the perfect marriage we find that when we allow Messiah to be at the center of our marriages, we are able to "marry up" into our heavenly calling as husbands and wives. Of course our earthly marriages include challenges and hard work, but we find we have an *Advocate*, a Counselor who always keeps His promise to provide wisdom if we sincerely seek Him. What a relief! What hope!

Katharine and I are very different from each other. These gaps cause us to draw especially from the book of Ruth, which Katharine aptly calls a story of "Love, Loss, and Legacy." God leads an outsider from loss into her promised-land destiny through her unfeigned love for her grief-stricken mother-in-law. Two cultures, two backgrounds, two religions, two generations become one in the harvest field of Bethlehem. When Ruth marries Boaz, the field owner, her quest for love is fulfilled, and she becomes an ancestor of King David and his greater son, Yeshua (Jesus). We believe that your life can also flow to an abundant promised-land destiny that is a part of God's legacy.

Perhaps yours is not an interfaith, cross-generational, bicoastal, (almost interspecies!) marriage like ours, but we know you ask the same question: can a couple overcome the vast differences we experience and enjoy ongoing unity, relative harmony, and joy? We can receive insight into this from Rav Shaul (the apostle Paul) in his letter to the congregation at Ephesus. In Ephesians chapter 2, he details the unity that comes from faith in Yeshua— how Jews and Gentiles can "find each other" in harmony. This great rift, one of the oldest in human history, is healed by the presence of the Spirit. He speaks of a new, or third, creation: *"one new man"* made up of Jew and Gentile. We may call this *"one new humanity"* in order to more effectively speak to modern culture. If God can get Jews and Gentiles to recognize that we are culturally distinct yet prophetically linked, how much more can men and women experience breakthrough in our marriages! He can do it for you.

In this easy-to-read book you will discover ancient Jewish wisdom for contemporary issues that will bless your marriage and home. You will find tales that encourage and lift your spirit to new heights. The principles within are time tested and psychologically sound. You will learn of Jewish marriage customs, communication skills, fighting fair, reconciliation—and especially—cultivating the presence of heaven in your marriage. As you implement the lessons of life from these pages, you will experience new levels of faith, freedom, and fun in your journey.

We hope to bring you a sense of how ancient Hebrew understanding can indeed have relevance for your modern-day journey. This book will help you experience some of the sweet moments of God's presence that can change your heart, your home, and your future. Drawn from my thirty years of experience as a Rabbi/Pastor/Doc, this book also features Katharine's wise counsel. She has always been indispensible to me in helping others into their destiny, and likewise she is present throughout the pages of this book. More specifically, you will find her sharing nuggets of wisdom that we are calling "Katharine's

Perspective." Our own mountains and valleys serve as examples of the sometimes-difficult but always-fascinating pilgrimage of faith. Each chapter provides a moment of reflection that you and your loved ones can implement, where I encourage you to "try this at home!"

As my grandparents would say: *L'Chaim*! To Life! ❖

Chapter 1

BOY MEETS HIS MAKER

"I'll shout it out from the housetops!" she announces between forkfuls of organic greens. "Jesus is my Lord and Savior!"

Oy vey! What have I gotten myself into? Here is the most beautiful girl I have ever been near, but she's a Christian, whatever that is. Still, those bright eyes, that perfect complexion, tanned olive by the summer sun, and her genuine sweetness are disarming. No! I couldn't let myself fall for a committed, cross-waving Christian. My grandmother would roll over in her grave—surely an uncomfortable turn of events in the congested Long Island cemetery where we laid her to rest.

"Do you even know who Jesus is?" she asks.

"Do **I** know…? **Do** I know…? Do I **know**…!?!" I sputter. "You are a great young woman, Katharine, but I have been seeking truth since you were seeking your roller skates. My quest has taken me through the religious paths of history. I have meditated in the desert, unearthed the secrets of the organic European countryside, practiced yoga at an ashram, and even attended a midnight Mass."

Katharine, on the other hand, was raised a nominal Catholic. She is a lot younger than I am and seems naïve. Regardless, I cannot get her pure-hearted, freshly born-again, faith-filled eyes out of my head. And I can't convince her that she is wrong.

+@#&*^%^#%! Myles, you are an idiot. Your pride is as tasteless as this mashed-bean, garden-dirt burger with secret (puh-lease keep it a secret!) sauce. On one hand, none of those paths you've tried has brought you real peace. On the other hand, she is so sincere. Enough hands! You sound like Tevye, the milkman in Fiddler on the Roof, *during his hippie period.*

"Have you ever even read the Bible?" she asks.

> *"Have you ever even read the Bible?" she asks.*

"Have I read…?!? I'll have you know I went to Hebrew school three days a week for years, until my Bar Mitzvah delivered me. I still remember some of the prayers (I think). Anyway, everyone knows that the Bible has been mistranslated and has come down through the ages as a bludgeon to keep ignorant masses in bondage to a powerful few."

She presses on. "Have you read the New Testament?"

"Well, no, not really. But I have read *The Aquarian Gospel of Jesus the Christ* and many other eclectic, profound revelations of the deeper meanings of that guru's teachings. Not everyone can divine the secret levels of these things, you know. Perhaps I could help you."

"Perhaps," she smiles, as her perfectly even white teeth peek through naturally full lips.

Across a Crowded Room

The above conversation took place only a few weeks after I first laid eyes on Katharine. That first moment was choreographed from above as if Jerome Robbins had permission from beyond to intervene in the lives of mortals. The scene was pure *West Side Story*. She seemed to glide into the crowded coffee shop lifted by the smiles and laughter of friends. I was ten yards away, leaning against a counter top, trying to look cool in my intense discomfort. Social settings had become stressful events. What was that light show—that glowing outline around her? Did time stop, or did I just stop breathing? And what was that painful pleasure in my chest?

Things progressed quickly. Coffee. A date. A walk on the hill behind my house. I wrote her songs. I was smitten. My friends laughed behind my back, but I didn't care. Little did I realize that Katharine was equally smitten with me. I was nothing like the tall, blond, inconsiderate Ken-doll types she normally dated. I made her laugh.

I also didn't know that Katharine had recently fallen in love with another man ... a man named Jesus. And she was determined to share this new relationship with me. She didn't understand the meaning of my Jewish background. She only knew that the more she fell in love with Him, the more important it became to her that I get to know Him for myself.

Katharine held strong values and morals. She was unafraid to challenge me! Once she said, "I dare you to be intellectually honest and study the Hebrew Scriptures to see if Jesus is the Messiah." I determined to enlighten her, to awaken her to the deeper things of spiritual life. I also made a terrible mistake. I asked "the sky" to send me guidance.

"The Sky" Sends an Answer

The next day, as I waited to attend an anatomy class at the local college, a strange man approached. He looked uncomfortably conservative in a golf shirt, tan chinos, short hair, and big smile. He told me his name was James. We spoke about the music playing on the stereo of my brand-new red sports car. Turns out he was a musician. In fact, he had played keyboards on tour with Van Morrison, one of my favorite songwriters. But this encounter was bigger than rock 'n' roll. My world was about to turn right side up.

The wind began to blow leaves through the parking lot as he said, "You know the real reason I came over here?"

"Noooo…." Suspicion mixed with curiosity welled up in me.

"The real reason is that the Lord told me to talk to the guy with the red car and tell him about My love. You've been praying for guidance."

He had my attention. *What? Perhaps Jesus was an avatar, an enlightened master, an ascended being, and an intergalactic guru*

Hebrew from prayer books. But in reality, I had no connection to Judaism as a religion. What was most significant was that, as a Jew, I was not one of *them*, i.e., the Christians.

Years wandering in the New Age estranged me even more from my Jewishness. As I read this Bible, I began to realize that my family line was significant spiritually. One side of my family was Cohen; they could trace their lineage to the priesthood. My Jewish identity leapt to the forefront, after smoldering underground for years in my attempts to be a stellar BuJew (Buddhist Jew).

To become a "Christian" was to become the most Jewish Jew I could be.

Through studying the Bible, God reintroduced me to my Jewish roots. It blew my mind, to use my vernacular of the day, that the whole story of the Bible, from Genesis to Revelation, was Jewish, and that to become a "Christian" was to become the most Jewish Jew I could be.

Nothing is more Jewish than following the Jewish Messiah.

I always thought Jesus was a nice Jewish boy who converted to Catholicism and became the leader of a Gentile religion for simple folk who weren't smart enough to know an "opiate of the masses" when they smoked one. My preconceptions were challenged by the entire Bible, both the *Tanakh* and the *B'rith Chadashah* (Older and Newer Testaments). It was alive and personally calling to me. The customs, the culture—the whole story was a Jewish one.

I quietly marveled. God knew my name. The words of the

Shema returned from my childhood, "*Hear O Israel: the* LORD *our God, the* LORD *is One*" (Deuteronomy 6:4)!

Not long after, my best friend and fellow New-Age spiritual seeker, David, stood a few feet below me on the concrete incline of our driveway. He happened to be toting a small clay idol that he used in his psychotherapy practice to help patients get in touch with their inner "spirit guides." I began to tell him, "Everything we've assumed about God is wrong. Jesus is the way, the truth, and the life!" At my enthusiastic proclamation, the idol's head spontaneously cracked off and rolled down the driveway. I stared in awe. David's eyes grew wide, yet the demise of his idol only strengthened his resolve against my newfound faith. Sadly, we soon parted ways.

Now I realized that this gorgeous girl of faith was right. I saw without a doubt that Yeshua is the promised Messiah of the Jews and Savior of the world. I came home to the God of my fathers, and the Messiah of Israel, Savior of the world, Yeshua, the One the Gentiles call Jesus.

Oh, and I decided to marry Katharine, the messenger sent by God more than thirty years ago to bring me back to the faith and the priestly calling of my forebears.

Try this at home: ▰▰▰▰▰▰▰▰▰▰▰▰▰▰▰▰▰▰▰▰

As you read this recounting of a meeting with Messiah, perhaps something inside of you identified with the wandering or the sense of being out of place in this universe. That's okay. Maybe you are an atheist, agnostic, occultist, spiritualist, alienist,

Buddhist, Hindu, communist, Jewish, Catholic, or Muslim, or perhaps you are entranced by some other "ism." Ask "the sky," the ceiling, your heart, the cosmos, heaven, or the void:

Is Jesus Lord? Is He the Messiah of Israel and the Savior of the nations? Say, "Hey out there, up there, down there, nowhere … are you who they say you are? If so, would you reveal yourself to me? Are you the King of kings, the Lord of lords … the Prince of Peace?"

Whether you receive an answer now, as you read this book, or later, we know that the principles within will enhance your life. But you need to know … the Prince does enhance the principles. ❖

Chapter 2

GIRL MEETS BOY

I liked Myles the first time I met him. He was dashing. And funny. And cute. His wit was quick, but never cutting or rude. He captured the moment and brought levity to the room. But more than anything else, Myles was kind.

I was drawn to the outstanding quality of his character, so superior to the guys I normally dated. I was a goner. But Myles was not a Christian. In my baby-faith style, I expressed my newfound love of Jesus to the man I loved the best way I could. Thankfully, God had already set a grand plan in motion beyond Myles and myself. Eventually, Myles met the Lord, and quickly we decided to start moving towards marriage. That road, however, was not exactly smooth.

Myles was romantic and adventurous. Yes, we had a lot of chemistry and were physically attracted to each other. We had fallen deeply in love with each other and with each other's hearts.

But we had also both surrendered our lives to God, to our greater call. We wanted God's best, and if God's best meant not being married to each other, well, so be it. We had to take a step back and put our relationship on hold to seek what God was saying concerning our futures.

I began dating someone else. Myles went on a great adventure working with Jews for Jesus. Life moved on.

However, at the end of each day I felt a little tug in my heart—a longing to tell Myles how my day had gone, to share my secrets with him, to laugh with him over my funny moments at work, to hear his advice. I missed my friend. I missed him a lot.

Myles, on the other hand, had my name taped to his fridge. Every time he opened the refrigerator door he prayed that I would find the person God had for me (even if it wasn't him). He was grounded, and completely non-controlling. He felt safe.

One afternoon, I began to ask the Lord earnestly to show me what to do. A decision had to be made one way or the other. The next day at work, the Holy Spirit answered me. While working at a school for special young adults, I grew close to Jeannie, a sweet, very high-functioning and sensitive young lady with Down syndrome. I had recently led her to the Lord, and was teaching her in Bible study. She stopped what she was doing, looked me in the eye, and said only, "You know, I like that Myles." It was one of those moments where you just know that the Lord is speaking.

It was time to talk to Myles. Needless to say, we were both excited. When Myles was ready to talk to my dad, he wanted to ask permission "old-school style," like he had seen in the movies.

He then decided to take my mother out for a picnic overlooking the San Francisco Bay. The meal was like a UN-level diplomatic lunch consisting of crab sandwiches (of course!) and hearty reassurances that Myles would provide for me and be faithful.

Overcoming Hurdles

My parents were openly concerned with the relationship. There was the age gap (Myles is older than I am), and there was the cultural difference. They feared that if I married a Jewish man, I might be persecuted. I was the first real believer in my family. Regardless, in the end, they realized how much we loved one another and that we were good for each other. They reluctantly surrendered to the inevitable fact that we were getting married.

I was the Gentile marrying their beloved Jewish prince.

Next, I had to break into Myles' world. Myles was a hot-ticket item among the single women at the Jews for Jesus base in San Francisco, and I was a threat. The first few meetings I attended there left me feeling like an outsider. I honestly didn't understand what was going on. While I may not have understood the culture, I did know that Myles' Jewish roots were important.

When it came to Myles' family, I admit I experienced a bit of culture shock. Someone had given me a prophetic word that I would be like Ruth to Naomi. I assumed this meant that Myles' family would love me right off the bat. Not so—my grand hopes were quickly dashed. I was the Gentile marrying their beloved Jewish prince. It took a lot of hard work and several years to win them over. Thankfully, Myles' sister liked me from the beginning. God provided one ally.

Now the only thing left was to plan the wedding. My parents would have preferred a San Francisco yacht club, with brass, marble, sweeping staircases and granite counters, swans strolling the gardens, and enough flowers to construct our own float in the Rose Parade. For Myles' family, NO wedding was the preferred plan. "Better you should wait for a nice Jewish girl."

We listened to our families patiently and decided to be married at our local church. We carefully added Jewish elements to a beautiful, holy, truly sacred ceremony. Friends wrote us songs. We practiced dancing the *hora*. I bought my dress. My mother cried. I cried. I was getting married! My life adventure with Myles was about to begin.

"*Therefore a man shall leave his father and mother and be joined to his wife, and they shall become one flesh*" (Genesis 2:24). Although there was pressure from our families to have our ceremony the way they wanted us to, we followed our intuition. For us—the delirious couple—we wanted to honor God and both sides of the family by incorporating Hebrew tradition into a modern wedding ceremony. The result was a unique evening that was memorable for all in attendance.

Try this at home: ▰▰▰▰▰▰▰▰▰▰▰▰▰▰▰▰▰▰▰▰▰

There is a reason we are telling you our story. When couples come to us in conflict or crisis, one of the first questions we ask them after we give them a few minutes to *kvetch* (that's Yiddish for "complain") is, "*Whom* did you fall in love with? Now write down the reasons you believe God (fate, destiny, the cosmos) brought you together."

In most cases, this has a very disarming effect, which lifts them out of their current complaint and points them to the foundation of love. Often during this exercise the Holy Spirit's presence is felt by all of us in the room. He, the Holy Spirit, is attracted to authenticity. When the foundation is sincere, the couple will relive that early love in a present-moment experience. We have consistently seen people soften towards each other and be open to the process of learning to love one another through the power of the Holy Spirit. At this stage, we are moving them from an intellectualized, rigid, critical attitude to one that is open to the ways of God.

Take a few minutes and remember your early love for one another. Speak out loud the characteristics that attracted you to each other. You will find the airwaves beginning to open and the blockages to love beginning to dissolve. ❖

Chapter 3

A WEDDING DANCE

"I am against this," my sweet little Jewish mother hissed under her breath. Perfect timing! I (Myles) was walking her down the aisle at my wedding! If Woody Allen had written this scene, no one would believe him.

I seated her in the front row of the little A-frame church in the San Francisco Bay Area. The mud-brown pews perfectly offset the worn, orange industrial carpet. Faded brown and orange hues were a relic from the mid-1970s. The sanctuary was a decorating nightmare, which had my mother-in-law apoplectic as well. She was accustomed to the finest things, and this was—well, a little funky.

Two for two. You are brilliant, Myles, managing to alienate two mothers in one service.

My Jewish mom was red faced at my seeming to veer so far from our Jewish roots. In the old country, New York, no one ever married in a church. Interfaith couples had the decency to elope to Las Vegas and let Elvis officiate. Granted, this was not your traditional synagogue affair. *But Mom … could you save your clenched-jaw opposition for another time?*

Here we were, though, and I knew everything was right. On the platform ahead of me was a *chuppah*, the traditional Jewish wedding canopy, which barely blocked the massive wooden cross on the wall behind it. *Chuppah*, cross, *chuppah*, cross … hmmm … this felt like opposing weather fronts gathering for the perfect storm.

Our Protestant pastor stood next to our Jewish cantor, making the best of a bizarre situation. They both cared about my bride and me. Our pastor, so blond, so blue eyed, so white he almost glowed pink, grinned from inside his trout-silver three-piece suit. The cantor wore the white linen robe of traditional Jewish weddings.

Our Protestant pastor stood next to our Jewish cantor, making the best of a bizarre situation.

Meanwhile, Katharine's family and their friends bristled against the modesty of the setting. They were veterans of high society and high-striving nuptials, and this brought a not-so-subtle smirk to their faces.

I didn't care. I was in love with an angel and the God who had sent her. I returned to my place at the top of the aisle, as a greeting and simple prayer of gratitude from the pastor began the ceremony.

So far, so good. "We're all in our places with bright shiny faces" keeps running through my head. How is it possible that a kindergarten rhyme intrudes at such a life-changing moment? What's next—"Play ball!"—or worse?

Suddenly, I was stirred by an unearthly chant in the most beautiful baritone Hebrew I had ever heard. The seven blessings for the bride and bridegroom mixed with the filtered dusky sunlight entering through the high windows. An atmosphere full of the palpable presence of the Holy One of Israel touched everyone. Peace—shalom beyond understanding—fell, and everyone breathed it in.

Katharine's Perspective: "I Love You; Keep Changing"

When Myles and I first met, we came from two different backgrounds. Myles is a New York Jew and I am a California Catholic. My parents wanted a country-club wedding and his family had their preferences as well. One day when we were out looking for the wedding venue, we were both aware that if we were going to make our relationship work, we were going to have to let go of our own old ways and let God influence us in the path of life that was before us.

On a twilight eve, as I was hugging Myles in the beautiful countryside of the Napa Valley, I looked in his eyes and said, "I love you; keep changing." Fortunately he wasn't hypersensitive and knew that what I meant was that to have a relationship, neither one of us could grow stagnant in our relationship with God. Thus our joke became, "I love you; keep changing."

We ended up not marrying in either of our family of origins' desired locations, but in a simple Jewish-flavored church wedding. We blended both of our cultural backgrounds to define the heart of the *"one new creation"* God is bringing together through Jew and Gentile (Ephesians 2:15). We honored Myles' side of the family with the *chuppah* under which we were married. We also had a cantor perform part of the officiating, and after we had *kiddush* (communion), we celebrated by stepping on the glass to shouts of *"mazel tov!"* The glass breaking has multiple meanings: to traditional Jews it is a mournful looking back to the destruction of the Temple. For us it also represents fidelity—that is, we broke our communion cup to signify that no one will ever drink from our love except one another.

Both sides of the family were equally uncomfortable at our modest church wedding. My parents and their upper-crust San Francisco Yacht Club friends were unenthused at our (non-alcoholic!) venue. Myles' side of the family graciously flew all the way out from New York, despite the cultural fear of not being welcomed. If you ask him, he would say it was out of respect for his dad, who died when Myles was a teenager. They flew across the country and set foot in a classic A-frame church with a big cross in view behind the *chuppah*. Nonetheless, there they were: his uncles and aunts along with his mom and her caretaker, who helped raise Myles.

When Myles' mother turned to him and said, "I'm against this," he wasn't sure whether she meant the marriage or being in a church with a big cross staring at her, or both.

To the shock of both families, the beauty of God's presence that fell on all in the sanctuary during the ceremony overtook the elite Gentile sophisticates, as well as the cross-country travel-weary Jewish *mishpochah* (that's Hebrew for "family").

Up, Up and Away!

"Baruch Haba B'Shem Adonai!" came the triumphant cry. *"Blessed is He who comes in the Name of the LORD!"*

That was my cue, as I walked down the aisle to await my bride. I surveyed the faces before me. Not a dry eye in the house, and we were just getting started. I snuck a glance at my mother, expecting to see the abominable snow mom oozing icy distaste. My heart did a flip-flop. Mom was weeping and smiling at me.

The bridal party took their places and then she appeared— the unlikely bride of Weiss, a heavenly vision coming slowly down the aisle. All arose, and the wedding march transitioned to "Amazing Grace." How true that rang for me; after years of lonely wandering God had sent me a companion for the journey.

I walked halfway up the aisle to symbolize the Bridegroom, Jesus, meeting His Bride (made up of believers in Him) *"in the air"* (1 Thessalonians 4:17). I presented her to her father. As I took my place, I heard him whisper, "Up, up and away," as he gently kissed his daughter. It was an inside sweetness between them; they sang that song together when she was a little girl.

The band kicked in with awesome original music born out of their individual stories of transformation in Yeshua. They were new disciples of Yeshua, having been beamed up out of the rock and roll universe. Accomplished singers and writers from well-known bands, they put a glorious personal touch into their song of love for God and for us. My keyboard-playing friend penned these words:

> *Dear Jesus, I present to You this beautiful bride*
> *And You know I want to thank You that she stands by my side*
> *It's a marriage made in heaven, a love that's gonna last*
> *And I know I'm gonna love her for the rest of my life.*

Our tag-team ministers walked us through the vows and rings, communion, and the kiss. At the conclusion of our ceremony, I stomped the linen-wrapped glass to shouts of *"mazel tov!"*

The guests repaired to the reception area, behind the stylish gray plastic accordion doors. We stayed at the altar for photos. My Mom and I danced the *hora*, a traditional Israeli folk dance. Our cantor sat at the piano and played songs of joy and celebration with a decidedly Hebrew flavor. This was quite groundbreaking—worship through dance was still a decade or two in the future for the majority of American churchgoers. The rest is a blur … little Jewish New York relatives munching like hobbits on radishes and roast beef … tall California Gentiles ("like redwoods!" blurted my mom), tuxedoed with gleaming orthodontist's smiles, gliding along to the sound of clinking silver and a string quartet.

And my bride, with that winning smile, radiating love and goodwill. Warmth and optimism flowed from her. Innocence and hope for the future marked the day. I was born again, again.

And Adam said: "This is now bone of my bones and flesh of my flesh." (Genesis 2:23)

The Ultimate Wedding Planner

God cherishes marriage. He loves going to weddings! The theme of His creation of the universe is the epic love story of His Son and His Bride. The spiritual history of mankind begins with a garden party and culminates in a cosmic wedding celebration. This is *the greatest wedding story ever told*, with redemption as the theme, and angelic choirs as the soundtrack. The Messiah comes for the one He loves, and together they rule and reign on the earth. No human wedding can fully represent the extravagance of that story, yet over and above the ceremony, decorations, music, guests, clothes, food, and wine, is the truth that marriage is essentially a supernatural act of Holy Communion and joining of one man and one woman in a covenant with each other and with God Himself. God designed marriage to show the depth of His love for His family.

As marriage and family counselors, we've walked countless

couples through their journeys. Marriage can and should be *mostly good*, which may include dizzying highs and devastating lows. But the Holy Spirit inspires us to open our hearts to allow Him to heal and transform us, and help other couples do the same.

God designed marriage as a place to worship, to serve and honor God by serving and honoring your spouse. Marriage protects against isolation and draws a husband and wife into a significant relationship with God. There should be nowhere to hide in a marriage relationship. Humans were never meant to live alone. All of our shortcomings, failures, and selfishness, along with our successes and joys, should be open and on the table. This truth can be both euphoric and terrifying.

A believer's ability to love like Jesus, to live selflessly and generously, is a key indicator of whether a couple will be in unity. Those who have been forgiven much love much (Luke 7:44–47). We have no right to cling to unforgiveness toward anyone, least of all someone created by God to be our partner for life. Easier said than done! But with the Holy Spirit, all things are possible.

If a couple draws close when offense presses them to run away, God will bless them with His presence and give them a powerful living testimony of love and redemption. They will reflect His image. They will enjoy the deepest levels of emotional and physical connection, and they will pass a godly legacy to their children.

Married on Purpose

Some believe that marriage is inherently selfish, and inferior to singleness and celibacy. That is not true. God designed marriage from the beginning. He blesses it. He says, "It is good!" Marriage, as created by God, runs on the fuel of mutual service and love. Holy marriages build families and communities, giving us the opportunity to sanctify, disciple, and develop Messiah-like character that loves in the face of obstacles. A solid marriage creates safety and brings healing to other couples, singles, and the community.

Your marriage has the power to touch the world with God's love in unexpected ways. Recently, for example, Katharine and I were privileged to appear on television with *Iran Alive* founder Hormoz Shariat, known by many as the Billy Graham of Iran. Every night Hormoz' televised preaching of the Gospel is beamed into Teheran in the Farsi language. To preach the Gospel or to become a Christian in Iran is illegal. The punishment for either preaching or conversion is death for men and life imprisonment for women. Young Iranians are fed up with their government and Islam. They long for true love, the kind only available through our God, who is love, and His Son Yeshua, who is the expression of that love. Amazingly, because of the courageous work of Hormoz and others like him, Iran may soon surpass China as the fastest growing (per capita) nation of believers.

Katharine and I had prepared to speak on the prophetic destiny of Persia. Shortly before we went on the air, Hormoz pulled me aside, his wise eyes staring intensely at me, and said, "Myles, they will be listening to your words. But they will be watching your marriage."

His words stopped me in my tracks. He was right. His audience had lived under the deadening hand of Islam and Sharia law for a long time. This is a culture where women are devalued, beaten, degraded, and denied equal access to jobs, education, and legal aid. The concept of marriage based on mutual love and respect, where a man honors his wife and treats her with love, while she respects him not out of fear, but because he expresses the love of Yeshua, would be a startling sign and a wonder. A marriage like that in Iran would have to be *supernatural*.

The concept of marriage based on mutual love and respect would be a startling sign and a wonder.

We were on the air for one hour. Both Katharine and I were acutely aware that we were living witnesses to an audience desperate for life and the love of God. We knew that because Yeshua is alive and well in our marriage and our hearts, the Holy Spirit would open hearts in the viewing audience and allow them to hear and experience the Truth. Who knew how significant a witness marriage could be? In His mercy, we came across as flawed individuals who knew how to forgive one another and live in love. Additionally, because God loves the Persian people so much, He allowed us to review the glorious history shared by Persia and Israel. For an extra blessing, I was able to call them upward as "Esther." Using my Hebrew name, Mordecai, I reminded them of their royal lineage, exhorting them to stand firm with Israel and their fellow believers in their nation.

The High Calling of Being Married

We might not all have the opportunity to be on television witnessing to thousands. However I will tell you this: there will be someone in your community, or at work, who is carefully watching you, wanting to see if the God you serve is real and alive in you. We all need to take this calling of marriage seriously. You are married for an important reason. Marriage was His idea as the first human institution God created. Refuse to believe the lie that your marriage cannot change or that you are doomed to a life of isolation and loneliness.

As you surrender your marriage, yourself, and your spouse to the Lord, prepare to be amazed at what He will do. He will heal every area of your relationship that needs healing and draw you together where you have drifted apart. He will help you forgive and be forgiven. He will fill your heart with love where love might have died. He resurrects the dead. He restores the brokenhearted and heals every disease. This is what Yeshua does for His Bride.

Our Heavenly Matchmaker

The wedding is only the beginning. Life begins after the ceremony. He has joined you together to fulfill His call on your lives as you walk out your days on the earth together. Katharine and I have been on this journey for three decades and counting. After raising two children and ministering around the world, we are still in love with each other and in awe at how the Lord brought us together. As a Jew and a Gentile, God gave us a special gift of experiencing the *"one new man"* of Ephesians 2, the Jew and

Gentile made one, in a unique way. The journey has not always been easy. Every marriage has its ups and downs, but ours has been unbelievably sweet.

Try this at home: ▬▬▬▬▬▬▬▬▬▬▬

Take a moment to recommit to loving your spouse the way He intended. Say the following words out loud with sincerity. Write them on a note card and tape it to your bathroom mirror. Do whatever you need to do to remember your resolve.

> *From this day forward, we commit to look for the best in each other.*
> *We choose to grow in love for one another.*
> *We will seek new mercies every day.*
> *We will be intentional, merciful lovers of each other.*

We are praying for you as these words are written. Yeshua, the author and finisher of our faith, our Bridegroom, our Beloved, is with you. ❖

Chapter 4

HEAVEN KNOCKS THE HELL OUTTA YOUR MARRIAGE

Why Get Married?

Did you know that married people are happier, healthier, have better sex, and live longer? If you are married, according to contemporary studies, you are "less likely to get pneumonia, have surgery, develop cancer, or have heart attacks."[5] Married people tend to enjoy better mental health, significantly lower rates of depression, and higher self-esteem.[6] A group of researchers in the Netherlands discovered that single people die younger than married people, regardless of the cause of death. In other words, your chances of dying from cancer or by homicide go up if you are single.[7] Right now, if you are married, you should pat yourself on the back and go and kiss your spouse. You did a good thing when you got married!

With that said, let's get real—there are many unhappy marriages. As a marriage and family therapist, I see this in my office every day. Tragically, there is no difference between the divorce rates in and out of the church. Believing and unbelieving couples alike lack the skills to make their marriages work well.

If marriage is scientifically proven to make us healthier and happier, it begs the question: *why are there so many unhappy marriages?*

The answer is found in the following *midrash* (ancient Jewish commentary on the Hebrew Scriptures):

> It is said that a Roman woman asked a rabbi, "If your God created the universe in six days, then what has he been doing with his time since then?" The rabbi replied that God has been arranging marriages. The Roman woman scoffed at this, saying that arranging marriages was a simple task, but the rabbi assured her that arranging marriages properly is as difficult as parting the Red Sea. To prove the rabbi wrong, the Roman woman went home and took a thousand male slaves and a thousand female slaves and matched them up in marriages. The next day, the slaves appeared before her, one with a cracked skull, another with a broken leg, another with his eye gouged out, all asking to be released from their marriages. The woman went back to the rabbi and said, "There is no god like your God and your Torah is true."[8]

Left to our own devices, we tend to wreak havoc on our spouses and ourselves. This damage is a consequence of living in a fallen world.

A marriage with God at the center of the relationship shines like a lighthouse on a dark, stormy night. Those who see the beacon are drawn towards the safety promised by its warm light. A measure of God's peace envelops that marriage. Friends and family describe it as safe.

After thousands of years, the Word of God still proves that when you follow its guidelines, God Himself will bless you with a sweet and abundant life. The Word of God, both the *Tanakh* and the *B'rith Chadashah*, are our sources of life wisdom. We believe that the Bible is the inspired handbook given to us by God. The Bible is clear that marriage between one man and one woman is "very good."[9] Our journey through biblical betrothal and courtship leads us to a place of deep intimacy, not only with our spouse, but with our Heavenly Bridegroom. Let's draw from ancient wisdom to find help for contemporary couples, by which we mean the wisdom found in the Bible. The best place to begin our exploration of this wisdom is at the beginning.

An Ancient Model

Let's go back in time roughly two thousand years and travel to the balmy shores of the Mediterranean Sea. You can hear the waves pounding the sandy beach, accented with laughter and singing. The aromas of salt water and meat roasting over an open fire fill the air. A crowd gathers around a young couple standing underneath a canopy. They have been waiting for this moment. The man looks triumphant and nervous. The woman's cheeks blush red. Yes, you guessed correctly. We are guests at an ancient Jewish wedding.

Weddings carried far more significance in ancient Israel than today. The ceremony encompassed much more than two people joining in love to start a family together. Significant social, economic, and tribal factors were implicit in ancient marriages. The cost of getting married greatly exceeded the wedding celebration. Grooms needed a hefty sum of money and gifts to pay for their brides. Arranged marriage was the norm. A young man or woman always married within the community or for the purpose of joining two communities together. Arranged marriages helped communities, protected their beliefs, customs, and property.

Does this sound unromantic? On the surface, one could conclude that marriages were merely utilitarian social and economic unions. If we dig a little further, the deep spiritual significance woven into the period of Jewish betrothal becomes apparent.

Yeshua's Bride

Astonishingly, the Jewish wedding mirrors the greatest wedding that will occur in the history of mankind: the wedding between Yeshua, the Heavenly Bridegroom, and the Church, His Bride. Before I continue, let me quickly clarify who Yeshua's Bride is, because of the confusion that occasionally surrounds this topic.

The Jewish wedding mirrors the greatest wedding that will occur in the history of mankind.

In Hosea 2:19–20 it is evident that Israel is the Bride of God: *"I will betroth you to Me forever; Yes, I will betroth you to Me in righteousness and justice, in*

*lovingkindness and mercy; I will betroth you to Me in faithfulness,
and you shall know the LORD."*

Paul later confirms this in his letter to the Romans: *"And if some
of the branches were broken off, and you, being a wild olive tree,
were grafted in among them, and with them became a partaker of
the root and fatness of the olive tree . . ."* (Romans 11:17). God has
only had one Bride: His chosen people of faith, from among the
nation Israel, as well as those grafted in—the Gentile believers.[10]

Whether Jew or Gentile, all believers are spiritually connected
to Israel, both "the ancient covenant nation and its modern
remnant," because it is God's desire for Jewish and Gentile
believers to be co-heirs and co-citizens in His kingdom.[11] Rav
Shaul (the apostle Paul) was very clear about this phenomenon:

> *Therefore remember that you, once Gentiles in the flesh ...
> were without Christ, being aliens from the commonwealth
> of Israel and strangers from the covenants of promise,
> having no hope and without God in the world. But now in
> Christ Jesus you who once were far off have been brought
> near by the blood of Christ.* (Ephesians 2:11–13)

> *I say then, have they stumbled that they should fall?
> Certainly not! But through their fall, to provoke them to
> jealousy, salvation has come to the Gentiles. Now if their
> fall is riches for the world, and their failure riches for the
> Gentiles, how much more their fullness! For I speak to you
> Gentiles; inasmuch as I am an apostle to the Gentiles, I
> magnify my ministry, if by any means I may provoke to
> jealousy those who are my flesh and save some of them. For*

if their being cast away is the reconciling of the world, what will their acceptance be but life from the dead? For if the firstfruit is holy, the lump is also holy; and if the root is holy, so are the branches. And if some of the branches were broken off, and you, being a wild olive tree, were grafted in among them, and with them became a partaker of the root and fatness of the olive tree, do not boast against the branches. But if you do boast, remember that you do not support the root, but the root supports you. (Romans 11:11–18)

This explains how believers in Yeshua, Jew or Gentile, are distinct yet completely equal. This blended olive tree, the wild child grafted into her older sibling, produces sweeter, purer, and more beautiful fruit than any other tree on earth. And she is the one that the Master Gardener has chosen to marry His Son. This union is mysterious, wonderful, and beyond human comprehension. So now that we are clear on the true identity of the Bride, allow me to elaborate on how her love story with Yeshua follows the order of the traditional Jewish wedding ceremony.

Let's go back to the wedding taking place on the beach. Our young couple did not meet at a singles group, Bumble, Tinder, online, or at a bar. Rather, the groom's father searched for a long time for a bride suitable to be his son's wife. Strange and awkward as it sounds to our modern ears, Dad was the matchmaker! This matchmaking process is called *shiddukhin* in Hebrew. The father could also assign his responsibility to a professional matchmaker (a *shadkhan*).

Those who believe in Yeshua were selected by the Father to be His Beloved Son's Bride. Just as a human bridegroom chooses a bride and she must say yes to him, we are chosen by Yeshua, but we must say yes to Him (Ephesians 1:4). The Bride, a glorious hybrid olive tree, is under a legal contract, a *ketubah*, with her betrothed. This document is the New Covenant or New Testament, the *B'rith Chadashah*. In this document, Yeshua promises to love and care for His Bride and to give Himself for her. The Bride promises to yield her life to Him and to Him only (1 Corinthians 6:20). Our bride's price is not just silver and gold, but Yeshua's blood shed on the cross.[12]

In biblical terms, the blood houses the soul. According to Leviticus 17:11, blood shed on the altar specifically atones for the soul. In essence, His soul atoned for ours. His blood took the place of our blood and sealed our new divine, unbreakable covenant with God.[13] By His ultimate sacrifice, we are set free from our former life of sin to live abundantly as His beloved.[14]

The high gift of walking alongside Jesus through life is a precious gift indeed and one we are unworthy of receiving. This makes Christianity different from every other religion. Other religions involve striving or ascetic discipline to reach perfection. Jesus did everything that was necessary "to do." Only through an act of faith (where we choose to believe what He did for us) can we enter into everything He has for us.

Both the Bride (the Church) and the groom (Yeshua) bathe in the waters of the *mikvah*, Yeshua at the beginning of His ministry with John the Baptist, and His Bride in the cleansing waters of baptism (Matthew 3:13–17; Ephesians 5:26–27; 1 Corinthians 6:11). Ritual bathing in a pool of water called a *mikvah* was done separately by the bride and groom before entering into the period of betrothal. The *mikvah* symbolizes spiritual purification.

Following the *mikvah*, the couple stand together under the *chuppah*, a canopy made of a prayer shawl. The couple publicly announces their betrothal, sealing their vows by exchanging valuable gifts, including rings, and sharing a cup of wine. One of Yeshua's last actions on earth was to bless the cup of wine, a critical aspect in the betrothal ceremony under the *chuppah*.[15]

I Will Come Again

Currently, we are betrothed to Yeshua. We are in the season when the groom prepares a home for his bride, and the bride prepares herself for her groom. In the Gospel of John, Yeshua tells us, *"In My Father's house are many mansions; if it were not so, I would have told you. I go to prepare a place for you. And if I go and prepare a place for you, I will come again and receive you to Myself; that where I am, there you may be also"* (John 14:2–3). Also, Yeshua pledges His love with an incredible *matan* (bridal gift). Ephesians 1:13–14 informs us that this gift is the Holy Spirit. In Greek, the word for this particular gift is *charismata*. The Holy Spirit comforts us in Yeshua's absence and reminds us that our Bridegroom will return for us.[16]

One of the unique features of the ancient Jewish wedding was the exact time of the groom's arrival. Yes, the bride and the groom knew the approximate timing, but the father of the groom gave the final approval for the last step in the wedding to begin.[17]

We know from Revelation 19:7 that Yeshua will return when the Bride *"has made herself ready."* Yeshua told His disciples that He did not know the day or hour of His return. This is not to say He does not have all knowledge. As with any Jewish bridegroom, He must wait for His Father to give the word that the set time has come. Asher Intrater, of Tikkun International, explains this picture beautifully:

> God does have a date in mind, but He determined that date by His foreknowledge—looking into the future to know when the people will be ready, or how much time would be needed for the people to be made ready. God's date is His date for finishing his preparation process for the people. It's like a graduation date—the important thing is not the date, but the finishing of the education process. There is a paradox here. If you are cooperating with the Lord, He will do everything to ensure that you are "complete" by the time Yeshua returns (Philippians 1:6). However, if you are rebelling against Him, then that "final exam" day will come whether you are ready or not.[18]

When the day does come in a traditional Jewish wedding, one of the groomsmen shouts out, "Behold, the groom comes!" and blows a *shofar*. Just before our Lord's return, one of the ruling angels will shout and another will sound a shofar in heaven! We will then gather together for the great wedding feast (1 Thessalonians 4:16–18).

Let's return to our wedding on the beach. The sun is setting over the Mediterranean. The guests, footsore from dancing and full of food and wine, are slowly filtering back to their homes. Meanwhile, our young couple on the beach gazes lovingly into each other's eyes. Joy, anticipation, and the feeling of setting out on the most mysterious adventure sweep over them. They belong to one another for the rest of their lives. Their future stands before them full of promise and new blessing.

This couple's story is not unique, and yet we love to hear their story and others almost identical to it again and again. This is why the box office loves romantic comedies that all have the same plot: boy meets girl, love prevails over all obstacles, and they get married. What is it about the essence of this story that we enjoy hearing over and over?

Simply this: stories like this are a picture of the greatest love story ever written. Such a story is taking place right now, and you and I are in it.

Undercover Lovers

One of the most stunning aspects of a Hebrew wedding is the placement of the bride and groom under the *chuppah,* which foreshadows the bridal chamber and places them squarely under the spiritual covering of God. Traditionally, a *tallit,* or prayer shawl, forms the *chuppah.* The *tallit* symbolizes the *Shekinah* glory of God, the weight of glory, and it is *only* under the covering of God's glory that marriage thrives. Hence the phrase, *undercover lovers* takes on extra meaning. Implicit in this play on words is the truth that we must commune with God to learn to live together filled with the unique and holy love that only comes from Him. Paul exquisitely expresses this idea in 1 Corinthians 13:1–3:

> *Though I speak with the tongues of men and of angels, but have not love, I have become sounding brass or a clanging cymbal. And though I have the gift of prophecy, and understand all mysteries and all knowledge, and though I have all faith, so that I could remove mountains, but have not love, I am nothing. And though I bestow all my goods to feed the poor, and though I give my body to be burned, but have not love, it profits me nothing.*

Without God's love, holy matrimony is impossible. The love of God is a powerful covering and balm, which covers a multitude of sins (1 Peter 4:8). Love like this is glorious. God intends for a couple brought together under a *chuppah* to experience the intense power of His love and glory. They are then supposed to release His glory through their marriage. Hence the sides of the *chuppah* are open to the community. Everyone in the community should have their lives enhanced, touched, and improved by the glory of God that results from the couple's union.

The sides of the chuppah are open to the community.

A fancy wedding at a country club at which I once officiated illustrates this concept. The wedding was between a young Jewish man who had received Yeshua and a sweet Gentile girl (sound familiar?). The bridegroom's family was pretty religious.

His maternal grandfather was an Orthodox rabbi. Needless to say, it was a difficult situation. His parents worked very hard, choosing to love and support their son's marriage to a girl who was initially far from their idea of the right kind of bride. The couple struggled in light of their parents' strong objections to the whole scenario.

Katharine and I had shared the love of Yeshua with the groom's family. They had even joined us at our congregation on occasion.

In the midst of the wedding ceremony, I did what I often do at weddings. I asked the father of the groom to stand. Then I asked, "Is it time yet?" The father of the groom answered, "Yes, it is time." While this serves as a metaphor for believers, it is also a beautiful picture for non-believers, illustrating that only the Father in heaven knows the exact time of His Son's return.

In this instance, when I posed the question to the father of the groom, he felt the presence of God rest on him, and he instantly knew without a shadow of a doubt that God is who He says He is. He gave his life to Yeshua then and there. The glory of God that emanated forth from the *chuppah* had rested on the congregation, including this precious man.

The rest of the wedding continued with a supernatural gleam. The bride circled the groom seven times, recalling the *tefillin* (small leather boxes worn by observant Jews for morning prayer, containing verses from the Torah) wrapped seven times around a man's arm. Just as his love for God is bound on his arm, so is his love for his bride. She took her place at his right side, a queen beside her king.

Their vows were solemn, honest, and sincere. The seven Hebrew blessings were read with more joy than usual. The groom smashed the cup beneath his foot with gusto that surprised even himself. The vows were recited and the rings carefully slid onto trembling fingers. The covenant was made. They were bound to each other for life.

Then as if a switch went on, the dancing began. What dancing! I think everyone danced until the stars began to fade. It was a profound start to a marriage.

More than one covenant was made that night. First, there was the covenant between the groom and his bride. And then there was the covenant made between the groom's father and his Heavenly Bridegroom and Savior. Each opened the door to deeper intimacy, trust, and life.

This is the fruit of covenant relationships.

Katharine's Perspective: Ali

When our kids were young we used to have birthday parties at the park so we could invite more people. One year, there was a young Indian boy from Fiji hanging around the party, so we included him. When the party was over, we noticed that he was still hanging around even though the other guests were leaving. He invited us back to his house and we saw that his dad was dying of cancer. We were able to lead his dad in prayer for salvation. Ali became a sort of third son in our family for a season. He would go to church with us every Sunday and then come back to our house to eat and play.

Ali is a beautiful gift to our family. His inclusion verifies the *"spirit of adoption"* of God and the Jewish mandate towards *ushpizin* (hospitality towards guests). *Ushpizin* is part of how we understand the *chuppah*, that the sides are open so that God's love can flow out to those around us. May we always be open to the outflow of God's love touching other lives for His kingdom.

Try this at home:

Ask yourselves:

What does the greatest love story ever told have to do with your love story?

Is your marriage covered in the Shekinah glory of God?

What can you do today to elevate the way you see your spouse? ❖

Chapter 5

BLOOD IS THICKER THAN WATER

Cutting a Covenant

What is a covenant? Remember when you were kids and you became blood brothers with your friends? You and your friend took a Swiss army knife, nicked hands, and rubbed the bleeding cuts together. Your eight-year-old intuition knew that there was power in the blood.

In short, a covenant is an endless partnership that cannot be broken, except under penalty of death. The Hebrew Scriptures are clear that a covenant is not something made, as in God *made* covenant, or Jonathan and David *made* covenant. Covenants are *cut*, which is the best English word to describe the process. Covenants are related to circumcision, itself a sign of a covenant. Like circumcision, a covenant brings to mind something bloody, personal, and painful.

Blood covenants were prevalent in the ancient world. Walking through a path made from the carcasses of slaughtered animals was a typical—and serious—business practice in royal land-grant treaties. Covenant keepers would walk between these sacrifices, making the physical statement that, "If I don't keep my covenant with you, let me be splayed open on the grass like these poor creatures." Consider how deep this commitment sounds to our modern ears, and how challenging to our modern hearts!

In Genesis 15 we watch the interaction between God and Abram (before he was Abraham). When the sun sets and darkness has fallen, a smoking firepot with a blazing torch appears and passes between pieces of bloody flesh. On that day, the Lord *cuts* a covenant with Abram. Blood is significant.

In the ancient world, when two people cut covenant, they would make a cut in their hands, rub the blood together, and then rub ashes in the wound, causing it to become a scar or a tattoo-like mark. All could then see that this was a person of covenant. The tattoo also declared to one's enemies, "I have a defender; I am not alone."

Yeshua cut a covenant with us. He bears the mark. It is said that in heaven, the only marred body will be the body of Yeshua. We'll be perfected, but He will bear that mark He endured for you and me. For all eternity, He has engraved you on the palms of His hands (Isaiah 49:16). All blood covenants between God and His people were fulfilled through Yeshua's blood, shed on the cross, sealing the New Covenant between Yeshua and His Bride. This New Covenant paved the way for the Jew and the Gentile to become one in Messiah.

The marks of a covenant include blood and a celebratory meal. There is a seamless connection with the way we celebrate communion today, going back to the Passover when Yeshua, preparing for death, gave thanks for the bread and the wine: His body and blood. Symbolism reflecting the bread and wine is seen in modern secular weddings. A wedding without a wedding cake and champagne is not a wedding! These elements remind all present of the solemn and joyful covenant that is being entered into by the bride and the groom.

Our obligation in covenant with God is to walk in holiness, so we can come before Him, lifting up *"holy hands"* (1 Timothy 2:8). In so doing we say, "I am in covenant with You."

Sealed in Blood

Back in the olden days when virgins married, the marriage covenant was ratified with blood. When the marriage was consummated, there would normally be blood. God created our bodies in a way that when a marriage takes place in the context He designed, a natural blood covenant takes place.

When a man and a woman are physically intimate, some interesting things happen. Powerful bonding hormones are released during orgasm, inspiring men to protect their wives and inspiring wives to bond to their husbands. These are the same hormones that cause a woman to be willing to die for her baby. We will address the power of these hormones later on in this book, but for now you should know that a single sexual encounter is sufficient to physically, mentally, and spiritually connect a couple for life. They "*become one flesh.*" The bond is so powerful that to break such a bond, it must be *torn* apart. There is no such thing as an amicable ending or divorce. There is only a tearing apart.

Anyone who has lived through divorce or had intimate relations outside of the marriage covenant knows the pain of being torn apart. This is why Yeshua states that God's best is that "*what God has joined together, let not man separate*" (Mark 10:9). This is not to say that under no circumstance is there reason for divorce. God's best is for a man and a woman not to break their covenant with each other. Yeshua argues that husbands and wives need to fight passionately to remain united *because God joined them together.* In one sentence He admonishes couples to uphold their covenant to love and cherish, remain faithful in mind and deed, to respect and honor, and to protect and provide.

> *There is no such thing as an amicable ending or divorce. There is only a tearing apart.*

In His wisdom, our Creator gave us marriage to protect us from the destructive soul tearing caused by sexual relations without covenant commitment. This is described by the Hebrew word *chesed*, or lovingkindness, that God promised to shower on us in covenant relationship. "*Therefore know that the LORD your God, He is God, the faithful God who keeps covenant and mercy [chesed] for a thousand generations with those who love Him and keep His commandments*" (Deuteronomy 7:9). His lovingkindness is everlasting as a solemn and binding commitment. Furthermore, this is how God relates to us, married or single, as a pledge of total loyalty. Don't treat God like a daisy, pulling petals off and chanting, "He loves me, He loves me not." Our commitment to love our spouses should mirror this security.

Covenant Keeping

In order to keep this covenant, certain relationships in your life may need to change. This is God's plan. Best friends, siblings, colleagues, etc., must take a back seat to your spouse. Ask the Holy Spirit if any relationship you have with someone else might jeopardize your marriage covenant.

Along those lines, the marriage covenant specifically insists that a couple leave their parents and cleave to one another, becoming one flesh. This is a design that God gave us to ensure the highest probability of success. Leaving your parents signals to all that you and your spouse are creating a new family unit.

When Katharine determined to go to Bible College, I helped her move everything she owned out of her parents' house. Filling up the bed of a borrowed red pickup truck, we created an uncomfortable but important moment for her mother. Katharine's leaving was a conscious act to separate her past as a non-believer from her future as a believer, and also as my soon-to-be wife.

Many of the issues we deal with in our counseling sessions occur when a couple has not left their parents, either emotionally, or physically, or both. Interfering in-laws can hamstring a young marriage and muddy the process with unnecessary pain and confusion. You might need some healthy boundaries between you and your parents to protect the intimacy you are building with your spouse. But that does not mean you stop loving them or turn your kindness off. Be sure you don't turn your *in-laws* into *out-laws*! Don't alienate your parents or your spouse's parents, even if you don't get along at the start.

> ### *Katharine's Perspective:* Enough Love to Go Around
>
> A new family unit should have God as the focus, with the husband and wife moving closer to God. In an unhealthy family situation, the family of origin may try to wedge themselves between the husband and wife. I have a classic example of how, when two lives are becoming one heart, we have to be careful that the family of origin doesn't try to triangulate in an unhealthy way. When Myles' mom felt threatened by me taking her only son away from her, she attempted to give him money to keep him connected to her instead of bonding with me. Myles, with a word of wisdom, said, "There is enough love to go around, Mom." That wisdom liberated me to feel covered by Myles, safe that he would put the new family first. It also liberated me to constantly reach for Myles' mom and make her feel included in our life.

You are creating a new family unit. Become the most secure, safe, peaceful, loving husband or wife you can be. This could mean putting the needs, wants, and desires of your spouse before

WHEN HEAVEN HITS HOME   53

your own. Trust God to take care of your own hopes, wants, and dreams. Stay interested in your spouse in the day-to-day. Be sensitive to their heart. Don't take your spouse for granted. Stay constantly in prayer for them.

I never want Katharine to feel insecure about my love for her. She is the most loyal, loving, and caring wife. I am at total peace in her love and loyalty to me, even though we can have fiery disagreements! Please note I am not saying that this sense of security doesn't take work. There are moments when you must draw on the Holy Spirit's love to show love to your spouse. We have access to a well of love that never runs dry. Thankfully, we are not alone in our covenant.

Three-Party Covenants

Picture a triangle with God at the apex. Husband and wife sit at the two lower points. The same principle applies to the walls of your home. Behind the walls are studs, which often have a triangular brace on them to keep them from collapsing. This third point of the triangle brings stability and enormous strength. Omit God from your relationship and you are left with the He Said-He Said Syndrome and walls unable to withstand the storms of life.

The third party in the covenant is critical. Many marriages seek for something or someone to be that third

Beware: there are numerous counterfeits ready to take God's place in the marriage covenant.

element. Beware: there are numerous counterfeits ready to take God's place in the marriage covenant, such as pornography, emotional dependence on a career or another person, or God forbid, infidelity.

For many people, the spiritual life in their marriage consists of prayer over meals and sitting next to each other on Sunday mornings for an hour listening to a sermon. That does not constitute including God in your marriage covenant! You must learn to share and pray together in God's presence while seeking wisdom to solve life's tough issues from the Word of God and the Holy Spirit. Failure to do so prevents a marriage from thriving and maturing. An extra bonus in this process is that as you move closer to God relationally, closer to the apex of the triangle, you simultaneously move closer to your spouse.

Early on in our marriage, Katharine and I discovered how vital involving the Holy Spirit in our relationship should be. Left to our own devices, we would have hurt and alienated one another. We can't lift ourselves in our own strength. Human nature gets in the way. We must have the fruit of the Holy Spirit to continue loving each other at this level.

Katharine and I have lived in the Congo and worked in remote areas in India. We've conducted marriage seminars from Hawaii to Siberia. I always joke with Katharine that I take her to all the "garden spots" of the world. But what happened to us in Siberia was remarkable.

Two hundred and fifty couples, each with a rubber-stamped communist marriage license, sat in the auditorium looking at us on the stage as we prepared to start the marriage workshop. They had no conception of the role of God in bringing a couple together, or His desire to become part of their marriage. These wonderful people had met the Lord, but Someone important was absent in their marriages: God.

Over the week, many miracles took place. The Holy Spirit rested heavily on the marriage workshop. Men and women experienced true repentance for spousal abuse. Some were delivered from alcoholism. At the conclusion of the weeklong seminar, we conducted a special marriage ceremony that joined God in the wedding covenant. The Holy Spirit filled the entire group with supernatural joy and resulted in grateful tears. A deep longing for something more was filled, as the Lord took His rightful place at the apex of their marriages. No one was left behind to go it alone.

What exactly are we supposed to glean from all of this? Ultimately, it is the importance of a covenantal relationship between you and your spouse, and between both of you and God. In the beginning, God said, *"Let Us make man in Our image, according to Our likeness; let them have dominion over the fish of the sea, over the birds of the air, and over the cattle, over all the earth"* (Genesis 1:26). Just as the Godhead is made of three persons, we are three-part beings, because we reflect God's triune nature. When you marry, you cut a covenant that is greater than the two of you. You enter a three-party covenant: you, your spouse, and God. *"Two are better than one, because they have a good reward for their labor. For if they fall, one will lift up his companion. But woe to him who is alone when he falls. . . . Though one may be overpowered by another, two can withstand him. And a threefold cord is not quickly broken"* (Ecclesiastes 4:9–10, 12). This is why we need a third member in our marriage: God. He is the One who enables us to "marry up."

The principles of God described in the Bible work whether you are a believer or not, because they are true. They are surefire ways to improve the quality of your relationships. However, principles do not come close to being in relationship with Yeshua. Think of it this way: the principles contained in the Bible provide solid building materials. Only a real, living relationship with Yeshua provides a solid foundation. Both the relationship and the principles are necessary for a house that will last through a Category 5 hurricane. The principles alone might get you through a rainstorm—which is great—but many marriages today don't last through a little cloud coverage. I would much rather have a well-built house grounded on a firm foundation.

Try this at home:

Grow your relationship with Yeshua. Don't let one day go by without His input and help. Let God be a vibrant member of your marriage covenant.

The marriage covenant demands that both the husband and the wife be faithful emotionally, physically, and spiritually. While these are promises made in the wedding vows, walking them out on a daily basis takes work. In the same way that we guard ourselves against the world to keep our eyes focused on our Bridegroom, Yeshua, we must protect our marriages by guarding against outside distractions that could pull our gaze off our spouse. Rebecca veiled herself when she saw Isaac approach. She kept herself for Isaac alone. We are to do the same with our spouses. Be relentless! Give sin no room to drive a wedge between you and your spouse. Do not flirt. Do not respond to flirting. Guard your eyes and your heart.

On the flip side, if you feel offended at your spouse's behavior with members of the opposite sex (intended or unintended), don't be passive-aggressive or hold it over his or her head. Keep the doors of communication open. Say, "Hey, Jeremiah, when you talked with Sara like that, it made me feel vulnerable. What were you thinking?" Give your spouse the opportunity to apologize or explain.

When you do mess up, take the humble route and apologize. Come clean. Repent. Pray with your spouse. Ask God's forgiveness. Ask for His healing. Ask that He will shut any door that needs to be shut in your life in order to protect the covenant you made with your spouse and with Him. Ultimately, ask the Holy Spirit how you should pray. Do whatever it takes to keep the covenant you made on your wedding day to be faithful to your spouse physically, emotionally, and spiritually.

You must rely on God throughout the day in every area of your life. I'm not referring to the old joke, "Excuse me God, but which can of tuna should I buy?" We don't look to God to displace all logic and self-reliance in the mundane things of life. I am referring to something I learned from my first son when he was still in diapers. When he got wedged between a large chair and the wall, he would look up and call out, "Stuck!" Taking a cue from our son, Katharine and I got into the habit of crying out, "Stuck! We need You, Lord! We need Your help. We need You to be with us because we're stuck!"

This prayer invites the Holy Spirit to be the stabilizing third party in your marriage. The Holy Spirit has never failed to help Katharine and me in these situations. The hard part sometimes can be taking a deep breath, getting humble, and praying. One of the tried-and-true techniques in chemical-dependency recovery is to employ the acronym "STOP!"

- **Stop**
- **Take a deep breath**
- **Observe**
- **Proceed**

I would add, hear the call of the finished work of Messiah today. Ask Him to be the third party in your marriage covenant. Discuss your covenant with your husband or wife. In which aspects of your life is God in the center of your marriage? Are there ways you need to live differently? Invite the Holy Spirit to renew your understanding of covenant and commitment. Ask Him to bless and rest on your marriage in a way that those around you will be undeniably touched and changed by the Shekinah glory of God.

Pray the following:

Dear Yeshua, we invite You into our relationship in a new way. We ask for Your Holy Spirit to convict, guide, and comfort us. We thank You, Lord, for the redemption we have found in Your Son,

Yeshua. Amen.

Jesus, be the center of our lives.

Jesus, be the center; everything revolves around You.

Jesus, be the center of our marriage. ❖

Chapter 6

LOVE IS A VERB

Life is not the way it was one hundred years ago when the fictional *Fiddler on the Roof* character Golde sang to Tevye on the Russian plains of Anatevka: "Do I love him? For twenty-five years I've lived with him. Fought with him, starved with him. Twenty-five years my bed is his. If that's not love, what is?"

(Tevye) "Then you love me?"

(Golde) "I suppose I do."[19]

I remember singing the part of Tevye as a scrawny sixteen-year-old wearing a ridiculously oversized Amish-style fake beard. The lyrics rang true to my young heart. I had the epiphany that real love is not always expressed in words or romantic moments, but in shared suffering, in loyalty and faithfulness, in the mundane of day-to-day life that only Tony Award-winner Jerry Bock could articulate.

Today, at the first sign of trouble or boredom, couples, once deeply in love, float the dreaded D-word and think about calling cousin Murray, the lawyer. Sticking it out like Tevye and Golde is a rarity. Few people really understand what it means to love someone anymore.

And yet, love is so important!

He who does not love does not know God, for God is love. (1 John 4:8)

"Love the LORD your God with all your heart, with all your soul, with all your mind, and with all your strength. . . . Love your neighbor as yourself." There is no other commandment greater than these." (Mark 12:30–31)

God created us with a deep need to love and to be loved. Why? God is love, and He created us in His image. We are touched, changed, and motivated by love. We live and die for it.

Loving well is essential. Learning to love is the number one thing we must develop in our lifetimes. When we stand before God, our wealth, popularity, influence, and possessions won't matter one bit. The only thing that will count is whether you loved God with all your heart, soul, mind, and strength, and whether you loved the people He put in your life.

Paul instructed men to love their wives, *"just as Christ also loved the church and gave Himself for her"* (Ephesians 5:25). Yeshua loves us despite our imperfections. His love for us is so intense He was compelled to die in our place. With that in mind, He is worth loving with complete abandon regardless of the circumstances— whether you are in a prison cell like Paul or a fancy mansion in

Beverly Hills. He is calling us to love our spouse with the same intensity and steadfastness.[20] This should be our consuming goal.

The Meanings of Love

Love suffers long and is kind; love does not envy; love does not parade itself, is not puffed up; does not behave rudely, does not seek its own, is not provoked, thinks no evil; does not rejoice in iniquity, but rejoices in the truth; bears all things, believes all things, hopes all things, endures all things. . . . And now abide faith, hope, love, these three; but the greatest of these is love. (1 Corinthians 13:4–7, 13)

I want to explore terms from two languages that do a better job of defining love than English (a language where love can be used to describe how you feel about deep-dish versus thin-crust pizza, and also how you feel about your wife). Ancient Greek and Hebrew expressions of love give profound insights into the multi-faceted nature of God's love—the qualities of love He wants us to reflect. We will see how these facets practically play out in our relationships. This section might get a little spicy. But God likes spicy. He invented spicy!

The first word I want to focus on is the Greek word *agape*. *Agape* is spiritual love rooted in affection, benevolence, and generosity. The term refers specifically to a "love feast of charity." *Agape* is sacrificially giving out of love. God's character is innately sacrificial. Yeshua demonstrated this facet of love during His final Passover meal and on the cross. *Agape* gives until there is nothing left, and then keeps on giving. It is difficult to love in this way unless we are empowered with the Holy Spirit. When our natural affection runs dry, we must turn to God for fresh grace to love. That kind of giving yields higher returns than withholding love. To quote the Beatles, "And in the end, the love you take is equal to the love you make."[21]

Agape gives until there is nothing left, and then keeps on giving.

The Hebrew word *ahava* is the closest word to the Greek *agape*. *Ahava* denotes intimate romantic feelings between a man and a woman. This word is also used to describe love in relationships that are not necessarily sexual, including the love of parents and children. The root of *ahava* means "to offer," or "to give." There is a deep connection between loving and giving. Giving leads to better relationships. Thus, the more one gives, the more one connects. The stronger the connection—emotionally, spiritually, and physically—the stronger the marriage will be.

Ahava is not just a feeling. *It is action.* In its purest form, *ahava* love seeks to benefit another. *Ahava* requires simple service: husbands give their lives for their wives, and wives honor and yield to their husbands. When Yeshua was nailed to a cross, His sacrifice was for love.

Racham and *chesed* are close Hebrew cousins to *ahava*. *Racham* is a compassionate and merciful expression of love towards the undeserving. *Chesed,* like *racham,* suggests the overwhelming compassion of God, and is an essential component to covenant relationships. *Chesed* also involves supernatural compassion, kindness, and mercy. It was out of God's *chesed* for Abraham that He led Eliezer to find Rebecca for Isaac (Genesis 24). Out of God's compassion, His *chesed*, He brought Katharine and me together.

Racham and *chesed* love keep you working things out at the kitchen table until peace is achieved. This love holds us together and restrains us from running out the front door at two in the morning, by helping us to express humility, kindness, and compassion, when pride and anger are the natural inclinations.

Racham and *chesed* sparked Yeshua with compassion to heal the sick (Matthew 14:14). They compel us to have mercy and compassion for our spouses. There is a divine and supernatural quality contained in these types of love. I find I must draw from *He Who Is Love* as the ultimate source of compassion and mercy in my expression of His love.

Ahava, racham, and *chesed* cover a multitude of sins. This love fills in the gaps in our characters that are different. Sylvester Stallone, as Rocky, quipped, "She's got gaps. I got gaps. Together we fill gaps."[22] God, in His mercy, created you with your spouse in mind. Cover your spouse's weaknesses. Be a partner and friend. Be merciful, gracious, and kind. Forgive much, as you have been forgiven much. Without mutual forgiveness, your romance is sure to wither away and die. Fill your spouse's gaps and let your spouse fill in yours. Truly cover your spouse. This is why He put you together! You are better together than apart.

Katharine has remained consistently kind through many of my emotional failings. My dad died when I was very young. I idealized him even though he was not an ideal person. My mother was distant and hard to please. I needed to be genuinely loved on a regular basis. One of the reasons I was attracted to Katharine was because of her lovingkindness. God designed Katharine to be loving and kind. She is perfect for me. The confidence she gives me from her steadfast love, kindness, and affection has become a place of refuge and rest. This deep love covers intellectual, emotional, and physical frailties.

Katharine was born dyslexic. I have spent a lot of time helping develop her reading and spelling skills. Today most people can't tell she struggles with reading and writing. For Katharine to know that her heart was safe in an area that produced deep childhood pain caused our love to deepen exponentially. In turn, she tries not to comment about my old insecurities that might cause me pain or embarrassment. I am not the tallest man in the tribe. Katharine never says anything cruel about my height. This makes me love her even more.

Though we will cover this in much more depth in a following chapter, you should know that when you do sin (err, violate, hurt, mess up … and you will), you should right your wrong as soon as possible. Check in with each other. Be humble. Ask for forgiveness. Be real, honest, and kind. If you are the one who was hurt, give your full and complete forgiveness. Create a place of safety for your spouse. Let your love cover their sin. If you successfully do this, issues that might turn into setbacks can catapult your love and respect for one another to new realms.

This happens only when we live in mercy, forgiveness, and kindness. God has the superior ability to turn weakness, injury, and personal deficiencies into something beautiful through *racham* and *chesed.*

Katharine's Perspective: Character

One of the things we have learned is that in a relationship it is easier to focus on what the other person needs to change, than it is to focus on God changing me. It is important to work on our character and not get stuck on being viewed as right.

In God's Word He has safety nets for us, and one of those is, "*Do not let the sun go down on your wrath*" (Ephesians 4:26). It means that you can get angry (and there are things to get angry about!), but we need God to help us focus our energy on the solution to the problem and not the annihilation of the individual.

In a healthy, growing relationship you need to work on character. What is the best way to do that? To quote our inspired elder stateswoman of faith, Hattie Hammond, "The one who makes it to the cross first, wins!" That was Hattie's way of saying that if we humble ourselves under the mighty hand of God, we will find His provision of the harmony that we seek.

Meet the Greek word *storge. Storge* love is familial love—when parents cherish their children and vice versa. It also signifies affection between believers. God teaches us to love one another as brothers and sisters. *Storge* love is the foundation of your "tribe," your *mishpochah* (Hebrew for "family"). This kind of love must be alive in marriage to build a real sense of family. Proverbs 17:17 reads, "*A brother is born for adversity.*" With *storge* love, we run to be close to our brothers and sisters who are in pain, which allows us to rejoice when they rejoice and mourn when they mourn, thereby providing protection, comfort, and stability.

In contrast, *phileo* love denotes friendship, attachment, and sentiment. *Phileo* love refers to the genuine affection shared between two friends who enjoy one another's company and make sacrifices to spend time together. *Storge* and *phileo* love work hand in hand to create a sense of belonging and joy.

Yeshua loves us with *storge* love, but what is amazing is that He wants us to experience *phileo* love *with Him*. He wants to be our best friend, to walk with us in the cool of the day and share secrets in the still of the night. This is why He calls us *"friends"* in John 15:15. Likewise, God created us to enjoy being married. The Amplified Bible states in 1 Peter 3:2 that wives are supposed to enjoy their husbands "*as a blessing from God.*" Husbands, you can take this verse as your own. Enjoy your wives! God gave you your wife as a blessing. Remember, it is not good for you to be alone. You have a friend!

The Hebrew words *raya* and *rut* roughly approximate *phileo* love. *Raya* suggests a friend, a companion, or a lover, (literally "darling"). *Rut* implies perfect friendship love, the kind of love we read of between Ruth and Naomi. In fact, the name Ruth is derived from the word *rut*. Ruth and Boaz' love affair is one of my favorite stories because it is an early epic love story between a

Jew and Gentile. Katharine and my love story reflects this perfect friendship love! Ruth 1:16 has become the theme song for our marriage, *"Entreat me not to leave you, or to turn back from following after you; For wherever you go, I will go; and wherever you lodge, I will lodge; your people shall be my people, and your God, my God."*

Your spouse is a gift from God to provide a faithful friendship. He or she is your partner in the trenches and this kind of love takes cultivation. Like any healthy garden, you must till, sow, water, and weed to yield a bountiful harvest of fruit. The fruit of this love makes life worth living. It cushions and heals. It nips issues in the bud that could fester deeply into roots of bitterness.

Katharine and I readily enjoy one another's company. When we first married, we learned to treasure every minute together. We never sought satisfaction in spending massive amounts of money on each other. We loved buying ice cream and taking a walk somewhere beautiful. As we are getting older, we are discovering new things we enjoy doing together.

Your spouse should be your best friend. This doesn't mean you do everything together all the time and only enjoy the same activities. It is healthy and normal to develop friendships outside your marriage. (I periodically play golf with a group of men or see "guy" movies with them—cowboys, spies, action heroes, etc.) Katharine belongs to a women's hiking club or meets friends for tea, and occasionally ... does double black diamond skiing! Having a spouse who is a best friend does mean you should regularly spend time with your wife or husband. If you had to choose one person to spend the rest of your life with on a desert island, it should be your spouse.

Because Katharine loves me and loves to be with me, she endures watching *The Godfather* too many times a year. Instead of getting annoyed, she pops the popcorn, snuggles up on the couch next to me—her best friend—and settles in for another round of the usual suspects.

Knowing we have a purpose greater than ourselves is what ultimately draws us together.

I hate to shop. I don't just tolerate it—I hate it, but Katharine enjoys the shopping experience. So I take her to the store to buy her something nice. It's a way for me to give. I try to help her pick out something beautiful because I know she appreciates beauty. In the end, she will look at me with loving eyes and say, "Thank you for pretending to care (about shopping)." When I hear her say those words, it makes it worth the agony of wandering through the suffocating crowds of our local shopping mall.

Higher Ground

Divine purpose puts every ego and every relationship in Heaven's perspective. God joins couples together with a Holy Spirit-energized mandate to walk together as *phileo* companions. For Katharine and me, knowing we have a purpose greater than ourselves is what ultimately draws us together, much more than our shared interests and hobbies.

Early on in our marriage, we set our course to provoke each other to jealousy in our relationship with God. Before we were engaged, my pastor told me, in his California-cowboy English, "Marry that chick. She'll pray for you, and you will never backslide!" We challenge each other constructively to reach for more of God, refusing to settle for second best. We encourage one another to follow God closely, forgive each other quickly, and move on with Him.

Nothing thrills Katharine and me more than to see people set free, healed, and filled with the Holy Spirit. We came from differing backgrounds, but share one thing in common: a commitment to adventuring with God. One highlight of our young life was a prayer meeting we held at our congregation when sending missionaries to serve in the far corners of the earth. We met at 5:00 a.m. before work, and later at 5:00 p.m. after work to pray for them. We would drag our bleary-eyed children and their sleeping bags to the congregation for the 5:00 a.m. prayer service, encouraging them to speak out in prayer when they were with the adults. They were raised in this atmosphere of Holy Spirit intercession. We would pray one thing on one side of the world and later learn of the correlated miracles God performed on the other side of the globe. This was long before cell phones.

For us, things like this are more enjoyable than regular hobbies. This is not to say that couples shouldn't play golf or tennis together. They should. Shared interests and activities are excellent relationship builders and lots of fun. However, the connection that grows out of prayer and walking out a divine calling together will elevate your love to a new realm of power and intimacy. That's what "marrying up" is all about!

Connection grounded in divine purpose will enable you to walk through anything, anywhere, anytime. Consider Yosef and Miriam, Yeshua's parents. This couple, perhaps more than any other, was connected with a mutual desire to trust and obey God in an unfathomable situation. They withstood the community's contempt for Miriam's surprise pregnancy before marriage, escaped genocide, lived as refugees in Egypt, and raised Yeshua in a nurturing home, so He grew *"in wisdom and stature, and in favor with God and men"* (Luke 2:52). They must have developed an incredible friendship of love.

Sex Is God's Invention

Eros is the next term we will examine. It is the ancient Greek word for sexual love. By the time the *B'rith Chadashah* (New Testament) was written, the meaning of the word had become so debased that the *B'rith Chadashah* authors didn't use it once.

Of the Greek philosophers, Plato was the first who believed that the human soul was trapped in a physical body. He taught that matter, including the human body, was evil and an enemy of the human soul.

In contrast, ancient Jewish wisdom, based on the revealed Word of God, is crystal clear in this respect. *God created matter, and it is good!* For Jews and believers, the spiritual life and physical life are inextricably intertwined. Consequently, sex in the proper context is not only good but also holy. In fact, God's first command in the

Bible is: "*Be fruitful and multiply*" (Genesis 1:28).

The most fantastic picture we see of the love between a husband and wife in the Bible is the Song of Songs, which describes the sexual, spiritual, and intellectual connection between a man and a woman. The Scripture paints a complete picture of a healthy marriage where a couple expresses the various aspects of love. It describes the emotional ups and downs and teaches the importance of quick forgiveness and reconnection after an argument. This love song doesn't back away from extolling the goodness of sensuality and romance.

Yada is the Hebrew word for sex, which means "to know." This indicates that sex is more than just a physical connection. Sex connects the mind and the heart, too. It is specifically a joyful experience of *giving* designed by God, not just for procreation, but to reinforce the marital bonds of love and build collective memories (to become knit together into one).[23]

The Hebrew word *dod* is the passion, romance, ardor, and fiery chemistry between a husband and wife. Used throughout the Song of Songs, *dod* means "beloved" or "betrothed," and implies carousing, fondling, and caressing. *Dod* is a pure, physical enjoyment of one's spouse. There is a reason why the Scripture from the Song of Songs, *"Ani l'dodi v'dodi li"* (*"I am my beloved's, and my beloved is mine"*), winds up on nearly every Jewish and Christian wedding band. Romance and chemistry are essential.

However, *dod* is simply one facet of love. If a couple relies on *dod* alone, the relationship can drift apart if the fires cool off. Real intimacy—physical, emotional, and spiritual—takes time.

A young East Indian pastor once told me that "in the West a hot pot is put on the shelf and slowly cools. In the East, a cold pot is put on the fire and slowly warms." Believe me, you want the pot that is placed on the fire. Passion blessed by the Holy Spirit stays hot when *ahava, racham, chesed, raya, rut, yada,* and *dod* are, without exception, growing and working together (which of course, takes time and work).

If you read the Song of Songs in its original Hebrew, the author appears to use different words for love seemingly at random. This is not the case. His message is that one definition of love is not enough to capture the passion within marriage. Each aspect is important. Your romance will soar as you creatively, passionately give to your spouse in every area of love discussed so far.

Those of you married for a while realize this is easier said than done! This begs the big question: How can you not only sustain, but increase romance until death do you part? A key is polite speech and rapid recovery from offenses. Recently Katharine reminded me of a public faux pas of mine that hurt her. I was able to "fess up" and ask forgiveness quickly. This moves our romance needle!

Try this at home: ▰▰▰▰▰▰▰▰▰▰▰▰▰▰▰▰▰▰▰▰▰▰▰▰

This may seem simplistic to veterans of marriage wars, but we advise people to treat each other as they would treat a stranger. You may say, "Myles, Katharine, I thought this was about intimacy. What could you possibly mean by this?"

We are glad you asked. We are commanded to love God and love our neighbors as ourselves (Mark 12:30–31). Beyond that,

Yeshua added, "*Greater love has no one than this, than to lay down one's life for his friends*" (John 15:13), and "*Love your enemies . . . and pray for those who spitefully use you and persecute you*" (Matthew 5:44). Yeshua gives no escape clause when it comes to love and forgiveness. If you are truly seeking to love Yeshua and follow Him, you will pursue love and forgiveness even when it hurts the most. What does this look like in real life? It means that we don't presume upon our closeness by indulging in bitterness and rage and other alienating emotions.

Try applying the same standard of behavior you would have for your boss or neighbor to your spouse. You would never freak out at your boss for small infractions, carelessness, or petty annoyances. You will be amazed by how politeness, patience, and mercy open the door to deeper conflict resolution. ❖

Chapter 7

WHEN WOODSTOCK MEETS NORDSTROM

L.O.V.E.

Husbands, love your wives, just as Christ also loved the church and gave Himself for her, that He might sanctify and cleanse her with the washing of water by the word, that He might present her to Himself a glorious church, not having spot or wrinkle or any such thing, but that she should be holy and without blemish. So husbands ought to love their own wives as their own bodies; he who loves his wife loves himself. For no one ever hated his own flesh, but nourishes and cherishes it, just as the Lord does the church. For we are members of His body, of His flesh and of His bones. "For this reason a man shall leave his father and mother and be joined to his wife, and the two shall become one flesh." This is a great mystery, but I speak concerning Christ and the church. Nevertheless let each one of you in particular so love his own wife as himself, and let the wife see that she respects her husband. (Ephesians 5:25–33)

A loved woman shows respect. A respected man shows love. Neat how that works out, huh? In practice this appears circular to many couples. Each one is waiting for the other one to demonstrate their fulfillment of this mandate. It is revelatory for them to realize that either one can start the healing in marriage by implementing what is taught in these verses.

When Harry (hypothetical husband) loves Sadie (hypothetical wife) the way Yeshua loves the church, Harry becomes willing to throw himself in front of a bus to save her. Harry would rather die than see his beloved Sadie suffer injury in any manner. Harry knows how much those little texts with heart emojis through the day mean to Sadie. He knows that she doesn't like milk chocolate, so he buys her dark chocolate (and not just on Valentine's Day). He understands Sadie needs him to listen to her rant occasionally, and then cuddle on the couch while she cries, instead of complaining about how emotional she is. Harry opens his heart to Sadie because he knows that when he talks about important things, she feels connected. He doesn't worry about sharing his heart with her because he married a trustworthy woman. Harry loves Sadie, a lot. He intentionally lets his love shine through every day.

On the other hand, respect and honor carry a lot of weight in winning Harry's heart. Sadie believes the best about Harry. She trusts his judgment and listens to his advice. She is kind to him, never haughty or rude. When Harry stresses out, Sadie is his biggest cheerleader. When Harry needs a little extra affection, she doesn't hold back her hugs and kisses. Sadie puts him before their children, her friends, and her mother. She does whatever she can to make sure Harry knows she thinks he is "the bomb dot com!"

Nothing makes Harry want to love and protect Sadie more than when he knows how much Sadie trusts him and respects who God made him to be. The more she respects him, the more he loves her. The more he loves her, the more she respects him. Harry impresses Sadie. Sadie inspires Harry. Harry feels like Jack Nicholson in *As Good as It Gets*: "You make me want to be a better man."[24]

Of course, husbands and wives need both love and respect. True love is respectful, honoring, and humble. Men just need a little more on the respect side, and women a lot more on the gushy love side.

R.E.S.P.E.C.T.

So what is respect, exactly? Think of someone you deeply respect. Imagine the person you respect *more than anyone*. Now ask yourself why you respect that person. Odds are, you respect that person because they are *trustworthy*. The people we respect are reliable. They come through every time. Yeshua never fails. He is reliable.

Proverbs 20:6 states, *"Most men will proclaim each his own goodness, but who can find a faithful man?"*

With most people, respect must be earned. You earn it through consistent reliability over time. How people treat you reflects how you treat them. Do you respect yourself? Do you love yourself? Are you kind, faithful, trustworthy? Can your wife trust that you will choose her above all others? Does she know you value her dreams, her opinions, and her heart? Have you earned your wife's respect?

There is a mystical element to this endeavor. As a wife, you can draw on the testimony of Abraham and Sarah, who saw God up close as He called *"those things which do not exist as though they did"* (Romans 4:17). This becomes a faith-led version of the secular "fake-it-'til-you-make-it" technique popular with coaches. The key is to draw on God's positive, life-affirming view of your spouse. Katharine and I were once following up with a couple that had come through serious long-term alienation from each other. Helen was a church mouse, always involved and doing extra service. Troy was a casual Christian, preferring golf on a Sunday morning to a worship service. They were living parallel lives.*

We asked Helen to dig deep and find the good that God had built into her husband, and begin to reach for him. Helen began to proclaim the "new" Troy and affirm him:

"You are really carrying this family financially."

"Thank you for being such a hard worker."

"You are a blessing to so many of our friends and neighbors."

Troy began to experience the overflow of Helen's church life—not religious activity, but the spiritual and prophetic call of God's voice, through his wife. He responded by wanting to BE the man she was proclaiming him to be!

---

* Names in all stories have been changed to protect privacy.

Troy and Helen found new commonality and harmony, and began to "tag along" to each other's events and explore each other's interests. They discovered a new level of harmony.

Earning respect is more like chess than checkers. The process may not be simple or fast, but is doable with time, patience, vulnerability, and healthy communication. The most valuable things in life are not free. Do what it takes to become the man of her dreams. You won't regret it.

The best place to start on the road to earning respect is a place called *humility*. You, a human being, may not always come through for your spouse. If you haven't already noticed, you or your wife might mess up on rare occasions. In these times, take the low road and apologize to each other. Ask God for forgiveness.

Admitting your mistakes and mess-ups to your wife speaks volumes about your love for her. This process builds abiding trustworthiness in you. The trustworthier you are, the more your wife will respect you. Take note, women—this cuts both ways!

Wives, how can you show your husband respect? As an experiment, try taking a posture of humility instead of an assertive "I know better than you" attitude. Be affectionate! Don't speak to him or about him disrespectfully. Don't second-guess him, stonewall, or push him away. Let him be the first among equals in your relationship. Trust that God gave you your husband for a reason. Believe in him, even in his weakness. See the gold in his life and call it out! *Even if your husband does not deserve your respect, treat him respectfully, as unto the Lord.*

One of the most reliable predictors of whether a marriage will succeed is if the couple believes in one another.[25] The Father insists that we want the best, believe the best, and speak the best about each other. Yeshua believes the best for us. No matter how much we fail, He calls us forward, encouraging, blessing, healing, and cheering us on. Do likewise for one another.

If you view your husband the way God does, you will respect him. And husbands, if you see your wife the way God does, you will love her. But the only way this is going to happen is if you repent! Repentance means to change the way you think, or to change your perspective. Ask God to change the way you think about each other, and ask for His perspective on your spouse. Then get ready for great things to happen!

Ask for God's perspective on your spouse. Later, if you run out of steam or don't know what to do, go to God and say, "Tag, You're it. I don't know what to do anymore. I need something fresh or I am going to make a big mess." He will, *without a doubt,* give you the wisdom and resources to solve the problem, heal the hurt, and patch the brokenness.

Katharine's Perspective: **What About Submission?**

As a wife, I pondered the meaning of Ephesians 5:21, where we read, ". . . *submitting to one another in the fear of God.*"

"*Wives, likewise, be submissive to your own husbands, that even if some do not obey the word, they, without a word,*

WHEN HEAVEN HITS HOME

may be won by the conduct of their wives" (1 Peter 3:1).

We are tempted in our modern hearing to think of this as an onerous kind of submission, but that is not the heart of the matter. I think of it as mutual love and respect. When I use the word *respect* I am thinking about the word *regard*—to keep his welfare in mind. I think about Myles feelings, not just my "honey-do" list of tasks for him. I look for ways to encourage the best in him and trust God with the rest.

Recently in a small group, the men were recounting their successes in ministry and business. Rather than compare Myles to their anecdotes of exploits, I gently reminded him publicly of a time where God had used him to make an eternal difference in the life of another. Myles was helping with a Gospel campaign in Bangui, Central African Republic. His young interpreter was a multilingual, born-again believer named Rene. This young man was grateful to have his job with our ministry, but it did not cover his bills and he could not support his wife and their infant son.

One night, Rene came to confess to my husband that he was visiting the mosque and inquiring after jobs for himself and his wife. The Muslims had oil wealth, and he was being pressured to renounce Jesus and join the mosque, in order to improve his economic status. Myles was incensed and said, "Rene, let's pray for a miracle in the name of Lord." They prayed together and several days later Rene came to work beaming with a huge smile. The sun glanced off his heavy black-rimmed glasses and he announced in gratitude, "Brother, I have been offered a job as an English teacher to an international family and my wife simultaneously got a position as a seamstress. We will be fine, thanks to the Lord."

This long-forgotten testimony resurfaced when I "covered" my husband in love.

I also find it is important to point out my husband's strengths in front of our children. We have two great young adult sons. They have been raised with my overt and verbal respect for Myles. Interestingly, they have said that Dad's respect for me has been an ongoing teaching for their lives.

Becoming Fluent

Now, husbands, let's talk about showing your wife love. We have a basic idea of what love means on a practical level. But what can you do to become a better lover? Just remember, men: God made your wives to need demonstrations of love more than you do.

Katharine and I have an eternal battle over time. I prefer to be early and she was raised to be fashionably late. Chronic lateness seems to have a genetic component. My mom was that way and my sister inherited the trait. My dad would stand at the foot of the stairs in our NYC home and shout, "Hannah ... please," in a vain attempt to address her "time-less" behavior. He would wisecrack, "My wife will be late for her own funeral."

During the course of our marriage, I "sanctified" this by saying, "My wife is like the Messiah; we know He's coming, but we don't know when." As much as I enjoyed this joke, I have adapted to help her in a more loving way. I can review upcoming events and go over the steps needed to be on time. It helps me to remember many nights in the Congo when Katharine would arise at 2 a.m. to fill our water buckets when the pumps were only operating for a few hours.

You may be familiar with Gary Chapman's five love languages: words of affirmation, acts of service, receiving and giving gifts, quality time, and physical touch.[26] Everyone experiences love primarily through one or two of the five love languages. Not only do you need to know your spouse's love language, but your own as well. The two of you may not speak the same love language!

Does an act of service light up your wife? You would be surprised how loudly vacuuming the kitchen can scream, "I love you!" Does she need quality time to feel connected? Grab her hand right now and go for a nice walk. Listen to her. Ask great questions, get cued into her life. Show affection, expecting nothing in return.

Wives, is your husband a physical-touch guy? Show him you love him by giving him a hug and a kiss and a back massage. Mark Twain once said he could live for two months on a good compliment.[27] Is your man a "words-of-affirmation" type like Mark Twain? Tell him what makes him the best man on earth.

Give specifics and details.

When Katharine was a young mother, at the end of a work day I made a point to kiss her first before I attended to the kids. As a stay-at-home mom, that single physical act filled her emotional tank to overflowing and simultaneously stabilized the children! They were secure that their parents loved one another!

Sometimes, just knowing your spouse is thinking about you through the day is enough to feel loved. The fact that Katharine was out buying shirts for me the other day warmed my heart, even though they didn't end up fitting. Meanwhile, I went out to buy her a Bluetooth device so she could connect her iPhone to her car stereo, but the price was double what a friend of mine paid. I called my friend to help me find the same deal and went home without the Bluetooth. Why? Katharine is frugal and loves finding good deals. I knew she would feel more loved if I waited to get a better price.

The idea here is that when we are out and about, we think about and care for one another. We fill up each other's cars with gas. We check in with each other throughout the day. We still hold hands when we take walks. These little actions add up big time.

One More Love Language

There is one more love language we need to mention that Gary Chapman doesn't cover—*the Word of the Lord.* The Lord speaks messages to us, through both Scripture and the Holy Spirit, that are intimate and specific to our circumstances. Remember that the Holy Spirit is the third party in your marriage. Sharing affirming, positive words from the Lord creates intimate affection because what He communicates reaches deep into our spirit. He wants you and your spouse to be perfectly connected on every level.

Let me explain. A friend of mine recently told me that he has been getting deeper into Scripture and spending more time in fellowship with the Holy Spirit, which has been a turn on for his wife. She was more affectionate than she had ever been before! When your spouse sees you becoming more intimate in your love with the Lord, he or she will be drawn into deeper intimacy with you.

Sex and Security

As we near the end of this chapter, there are two other facets of love between a husband and wife we should discuss: sex and security. Most men need sex more than their wives. Likewise, more than husbands, most women need to feel a sense of protection and safety. Sex and security translate into love and respect for men and women respectively.

Let's switch gears for a minute and have a quick review of your high school sex-ed class. You're over twenty-one. You can handle it. Your sex drive creates emotional, physical, and mental bonds for life with your spouse. These bonds intensify each time you are intimate. Sex releases dopamine and serotonin, called the "happy endorphins." These chemicals signal pleasure and increase concentration. Dopamine specifically is a reward chemical. Hence, you will want to have sex again and again. It is easy to see that God wants this chemical released so that throughout your marriage you will want to connect again and again with your spouse.[28]

Oxytocin is another chemical that appears on the scene. Oxytocin is the trust-and-bonding hormone that plays a role primarily in the woman. It attaches her emotionally to her husband and children. For men, the primary hormone released in sex is vasopressin. Vasopressin is a commitment hormone. Essentially, the woman has a special nurturing hormone, while the man has a special protective/preserving hormone, released in sex. These beautiful gifts encourage a man to give up everything for his wife, and a woman to desire only her husband. Sounds a lot like Ephesians 5:25–33, doesn't it?[29]

This is profound. Sex inspires the man to protect and stay loyal to his wife. The protected wife feels secure—hence, loved. The loved woman responds positively to her husband's care. He, in turn, feels respected. This deepens their bond, they both receive and give love, and the cycle continues.

What exactly can a man do to make his wife feel protected and secure? It is not primarily about wealth, but it is about *commitment*. Whether you sell yachts or flip hamburgers, your wife needs to know that you are committed to doing whatever you need to do to care for her and the children.

The other side of the security coin is fidelity. Don't chase or even flirt with other women and cause your wife to feel insecure about your love. Nothing damages a marriage more than infidelity. This applies equally to women.

Find out what makes your wife feel secure. Then make her feel secure. Do what it takes. Believe me, you will see serious improvement in your sex life!

God designed men to want to connect sexually with their wives on average every three days. Women, on the other hand, are on a twenty-eight-day cycle. Depending on where they are in that cycle, different responses will be produced.

Every few days a husband is extra-inspired to be kind to his wife, knowing that a loved woman responds better to his, "Are you awake, Babe?" This is a God-given way to protect the marriage covenant and continually deepen the connection between a husband and wife.

Women, don't think that when your husband wants to be intimate with you that he only wants you for your body. This is not mercenary. *This is God's design!*

Beyond connecting on a regular basis, God's plan for a healthy sexual partnership provides a unique environment to practice loving well. Mutual self-sacrifice and giving is required, which means a woman says yes even when she doesn't feel like it, and a husband is sensitive to his wife's physical, emotional, and spiritual needs. The fruit is respected husbands and beloved wives. Furthermore, this meets a man's God-given need for regular physical intimacy and a woman's need for security.

Got to Have All Your Loving!

Emotions and people should not dictate when we love. We love out of obedience. If we love Yeshua, we will keep His commandment to love one another. We have the option to choose love no matter how our spouse behaves. The Lord counts this as worship.[30]

If your spouse seems unlovable, angry, and distant, love them.

Respect them. Don't let your love or respect rest tenuously on their behavior towards you. Yeshua's love for you is not dependent on your behavior. When Yeshua said He loved us, He meant it. He loves us, completely, totally, all the time. When we don't love Him back, He still loves us. He loves us when we are not spiritual, victorious, or strong—He loves us regardless.[31] Respond the same with your spouse. Love your husband when he is not spiritual. Love your wife when she fails. Love in your spouse's weakness. Love the same way the Lord loves you.

We have the option to choose love no matter how our spouse behaves.

As the years progress, finding new ways of romancing your spouse can be fun. Even in writing this, Katharine and I realized that it was a good time to check in and see how we were doing loving one another. We asked what it means to partner in love with each other in new and loving ways. We asked what we could do to step up our game. We redefined romance and sexuality, even at this stage in our life.

Try this at home:

All of us need to ask God, ourselves, and each other what the next phase of love should look like. Friendship, mercy, kindness, a healthy sex life, selflessness, sacrifice, and generosity integrate to make a lifelong connection. Don't let a single one of these hot elements grow cold.

Communication is key. Speak what's unspoken. Talk with

each other about love, respect, security, and sex. When did you last go out for a real date? Are you spending enough time being intimate? Have you been too distracted by work or children? How can you become more giving? What needs do you need met? Do you need to forgive or ask forgiveness?

Ask yourself, "What would be a blessing for us to do together?" Then provide a way to bless your spouse. I can't afford a sailboat, but I can take my wife out on San Francisco Bay with friends who do skipper one. Hiking, an occasional movie out, walking the dog, working in the yard together, visiting friends, riding bikes, are all low-cost, easy ways to build positive times together. Cultivating physical intimacy (keeping your sex life alive!) also takes the rough edges off the relationship.

Do not shy away from these topics. The more comfortable you become speaking about uncomfortable areas, the healthier your marriage will become.

Katharine and I want to challenge you to more fully love one another. Go to the Holy Spirit for fresh inspiration on loving well. Ask Him for a fresh revelation of His love for you. His presence will overflow into your love life as you spend time with Him. Don't leave the Holy Spirit out of your relationship and romance.

On that note, shut this book, find your spouse, and give him or her a long tender kiss. Then, express your *love* to your spouse in a special way. ❖

Chapter 8

CHECK YOUR BAGGAGE AT THE DOOR

The Handicaps We Bring to Our Marriages

My teachers in grade school labeled me. Based on reading comprehension and math scores, they took six of us from the second grade and advanced us to fourth grade. However, the school officials didn't take into consideration certain drawbacks. I was shorter than everyone, and the skipped grade separated me from lifelong neighborhood friends. As a result, I suffered emotionally and a sense of alienation took root in my psyche. After my bar mitzvah, experimentation with drugs and alcohol became a lifestyle. I spent my junior year of high school at the local racetrack; gambling with stolen money or cash I won playing poker. My dad found out when the school called and said I was not going to become a senior! He said to me, "If I catch you at the race track again, I will cut your legs off and you will be the best jockey in town." The school made him an offer he could not refuse. If his prodigal son could pass all his finals, they would allow him to become a senior. My dad swung into action and forced me to spend my days studying for my finals at his factory. Although a captive, I actually enjoyed driving to work every day with my dad. I passed all of my classes. The school strongly recommended that I be sent to a private school for my senior year.

Always feeling a step or two behind my classmates back home added to my sense of alienation. I began my senior year in Massachusetts at a fancy-pants private school and lasted almost a semester. I was kicked out and completed the spring semester at another prep school further north in Maine, from which I gratefully graduated. At the rate I was going in my doggedly consistent northern trek, I think my parents worried I would end up a Canadian Mountie!

Miraculously, I was accepted at Clark University and decided to study psychology, believing that it would help me sort out my life and understand my dysfunctional family. My choice was based on the fact that Freud and Jung lectured there on an American tour. On the first day of freshman orientation, an upper classman hippie offered me some weed and choked out a smoke-filled phrase, "Today we're having a freshman 'disorientation' on the hill." That was music to my ears and kicked off my college career and subsequent "magical misery tour." Drugs, alcohol, and eventually New Age philosophy led me further down the rabbit hole of alienation. From yoga ashrams to desert meditations to pot farming in my "back to the land" moment on Cape Cod, I was painfully adrift.

Katharine had a different experience. She was dyslexic, so school was a different kind of torture. She learned to fake her way through the public education system. There was no opportunity to learn phonics or the many other tools that help students with reading disabilities today. Katharine is brilliant emotionally and relationally. She often understands how and why people think and act the way they do. That is one of the reasons she is such an asset to me as a co-counselor, TV co-host, tour leader, and minister.

However, our personal differences were vast, starting with our age. Our music, literature, movies and TV, and cultural references were from two different generations. If two people as diverse as Katharine and I can stay committed while constantly looking for the best in each other, most any couple can make it in life.

United We Stand

I remember our first mini-conflict, which took place during our honeymoon. For one week we experienced a state of romantic heaven. Suntanned and blissfully unaware of what married life is really like, we walked through the door of our tiny little apartment and right into our first argument. Katharine expected that we would walk in the door and continue our oasis of love, just the two of us. Instead, I went to

We walked through the door of our tiny little apartment and right into our first argument.

visit some of the guys from Bible College. While this wasn't a bad idea in and of itself, my new wife read it as rejection. She felt vulnerable, ignored, and insecure.

We vowed to work it (whatever "it" was) through, no matter what. Somehow, we knew that a commitment to work through difficulties and conflict to stay joined together was synonymous with love and becoming one flesh.

Even in our first weeks of marriage, we knew we needed to invite God's wisdom into our conflicts. That meant sitting in two director's chairs in the corner of our living room and talking and praying issues through to resolution. We each received wisdom and healing in this way; I became aware of Katharine's sensitivity and she learned to be confident in my motivation. This is an important lesson. Some wise guy said, "In order for a fire to burn well, there needs to be some space between the logs. Too much space and the fire goes out. Too little space and the fire is smothered." In a similar fashion, couples need to learn to enjoy the rhythm of being together and being apart without doubting their love or commitment.

When Yeshua said, "*So then they are no longer two, but one flesh. Therefore what God has joined together, let not man separate*" (Mark 10:8-9), the lesson was to not separate. Even when you think it is inevitable. Of course, this extends beyond your marriage to family and community. Consider Paul's words to the Corinthians, "*Now I plead with you, brethren, by the name of our Lord Jesus Christ, that you all speak the same thing, and that there be no divisions among you, but that you be perfectly joined together in the same mind and in the same judgment"* (1 Corinthians 1:10). God mandates the pursuit of unity in love.

Here's a fact of life: if you marry, you will have conflict. Our ability to understand and communicate perfectly was lost in the fall of mankind. We are broken people! But the Lord God is eager to restore us and teach us how to handle conflicts constructively. He wants to transform us into His image, and if we yield to His instructive voice, our relationship will thrive and prosper. If not, we risk reaping the negative rewards of mismanaged anger, festering bitterness, pride, and unforgiveness.

Resolving conflict takes work and practice (we will cover this more in depth in a later chapter). When conflict erupts, don't pull out your big guns and start shooting. Discipline yourself to disagree while maintaining an entreating spirit. Katharine and I work hard not to criticize or show contempt for each other, instead we focus on diffusing anger and seeking *shalom*. Communicate in a framework that speaks life and not condemnation, such as suggesting how we can "do better next time." Your spouse may not be open to change, but God can bring issues back around and open your minds to new strategies.

Finally, accept that your partner is human and will never be perfect. Neither will you be, for that matter. With that in mind, be realistic about showing grace where grace is needed. Ask yourself if it is that big a deal if your spouse is consistently late to the airport or talks too long on the phone. You have your unique issues. One way or another, problems like that are easily solved without escalating into World War III, by applying more grace and less selfishness. In short, be an adult, dialogue, compromise, change your behavior if you need to move on, and don't look back.

Divided We Fall

There are relational factors that, if evident in your relationship, point to a high probability of division and divorce. These include unchecked selfishness and pride, petty grievances that grow into irrational blow-ups, unhealed childhood trauma, disrespect and dishonor for your partner, divergent views on spending or child rearing. The list goes on. *"The thief does not come except to steal, and to kill, and to destroy"* (John 10:10). He will exploit these weaknesses in your relationship if you give him permission to do so through disobedience to the Word.

In recognizing the factors attacking the foundation of your marriage, you can begin to repair the damage proactively and get back on course. If you are having difficulty seeing clearly, you might consider seeking help from a trained counselor or wise friend.

Katharine's Perspective: Don't Quench His Gift!

I fell in love with Myles partly because of his music, which revealed his heart. He wrote romantic songs and sang to me in his lovely singing voice. He would often play his guitar between counseling sessions to refocus on the Holy Spirit and when he got home, to help him process the day.

A few years into our married life, I became focused

on changing diapers, cleaning the house, and a garden full of weeds. One afternoon, Myles was sitting alone in the room playing music. I couldn't hear the song. The only thing I could hear was the resentful voice in my head accusing him of not helping me with the kids or weeding the garden in that moment. In all fairness, Myles would help me with the kids and around the house at other times of the day.

Subconsciously, I was quenching the gifting in Myles with my resentful thoughts that he should put the guitar down and get busy helping me. This issue repeatedly resurfaced and caused a lot of pain on both sides. I had stepped into the harsh taskmaster syndrome that affects so many women. Then when I saw the guitar sitting in the corner and Myles' voice no longer filled the house, I realized what I had done. Thankfully, it was early on in our marriage, and I was able to avoid crushing his musical gift.

When it comes to having a good marriage, you have to allow the Holy Spirit to be your counselor. If you don't, you will slowly erode your relationship. When you feel the Holy Spirit convict you of something you need to apologize for, do it! Don't wait until you have shut down your spouse's gifting or hurt each other beyond repair.

The Importance of Forgiveness

The release of forgiveness is the strongest aphrodisiac in the book.

Consider God's forgiveness towards us as sinners.

Consider God's forgiveness towards us as sinners. His mercy awakens a profound love for Him. It works similarly with our spouse. Forgiveness is a central pillar of a marriage steeped in faith. It is the application of the love of God that heals deep wounds and resurrects the flatlined heart. One of the most powerful things we can do to stay in and cultivate love is to live in continual and mutual forgiveness.

Keeping romance alive is innately connected to forgiveness. Changing your actions towards your spouse is easy. If you as a husband need to pursue her again, make date night a priority. If you as a wife need to become less controlling and more giving, you can trim your attitude. If you both need to think more positively and criticize less, you can hold each other accountable. These changes are straightforward and doable, but they are impossible if someone is clinging to a backlog of offense. Hence, you need to stay up to date forgiving one another. Move from an intellectual understanding of forgiveness to one that is deeply felt. This gives the life of your marriage a chance to grow. Close the door on the enemy and refuse to keep long accounts and grudges.

This does not mean that if your spouse has done something wrong that they should not be corrected. They should. However, your forgiveness is not based on their behavior, but rather is based on Yeshua's command to forgive the same way He forgave you. The ramifications of unearned forgiveness go way beyond your marriage.

WHEN HEAVEN HITS HOME   101

When Lou Engle asked me to help lead communion at the
Berkeley Call in 2014, I was to partner with a young Native
American. Lou's idea was to do the service at 3:00 p.m., the
same time of day that Yeshua died, shedding His blood for us. In
speaking with my communion co-leader, I attempted to divide
the ministry evenly between us so that neither would have
more prominence over the other. This wise young man insisted,
"Brother, I only have one word." I continued harassing him in
love and he repeated, "Brother, God has only given me one word."

Our time in the service came, and I did my part in Hebrew
and in English. It was well received, and then my co-leader stood
up and said, "I have a word for my Native American brothers, my
African American brothers, my Asian American brothers, my
Hispanic American brothers, and all the women gathered here.
It is time to offer forgiveness without an apology."

Needless to say, the anointing of the Lord multiplied and lifted
everyone into a new place.

Try this at home:

We are called to reconcile ourselves to God and to others, and
to forgive those who have wronged us. Once you have sought
forgiveness from Yeshua, you need to ask forgiveness from your
spouse, your friends, your boss, or whomever you have wronged.
Believe me, every person—married or single—needs to learn
how to say "*I am sorry*," and "*I forgive you*." It will set you free
from guilt and shame, and will release you to heal.

If you are asking forgiveness and follow these steps without sincerity, you will betray your spouse's trust. Don't speak empty words. Follow through! Forgiveness must be specific. When we actually walk in the other's shoes, when we understand how we hurt one another, it is as if a little understanding of God is released. There is an exchange that is priceless and a reflection of God's exchange with us when He gave His Son for us.

Katharine and I follow Lori and Barry Byrne's five steps to reconciliation when we need to ask for forgiveness.[32] We say the following and fill in the blank as specifically as possible:

1. This (fill in the blank) is what I did wrong to hurt you.
2. This (fill in the blank) is the pain that I believe I caused you.
3. This (fill in the blank) is how I feel now about causing you that pain.
4. This (fill in the blank) is my commitment not to bring that pain into our marriage in the future.
5. Will you forgive me for causing you this pain?

If you are on the receiving side, forgive completely. Let go. Do not hold your spouse's failure in your back pocket to use as a weapon at a later time. Unforgiveness devastates relationships and fertilizes roots of bitterness. You need to forgive your spouse even if they don't apologize. If you do not, your Heavenly Father will not forgive you (Matthew 6:14–15). ❖

Chapter 9

BELIEVING FOR THE BEST

He Ain't Heavy, He's My Brother

A story about Rabbi Aryeh Levin, the famous nineteenth-century *Tzaddik* (Jewish saint) of Jerusalem, speaks of shared suffering in his marriage. The rabbi took his wife to the doctor and explained, "My wife's foot is hurting us."[33] In a single phrase, the rabbi revealed what marriage is all about: a shared reality with another human being. Your spouse's pain becomes yours. Your wounds become your spouse's.[34]

Neither of you may have sore feet, but odds are you suffer somewhere in your bodies or in your hearts. Your shared approach towards pain and suffering holds the power either to drive a wedge in your relationship or to pull you closer together in intimacy.

Katharine's Perspective: Dhanbad

Myles was in Dhanbad, India, setting up a pastor's conference and open-air public Gospel meetings. The city was a hotbed of the BJP, an extremist political party that wanted India for Indians only, viewing Christianity as a threat to indigenous Indian life. They were vehemently anti-Christian. There were threats on the workers' lives while they were setting up the grounds and the school of ministry. This was in pre-cell phone days. We had only occasional faxes, but fax machines were hard to get to over in India. I prayed night and day in California with our ladies' intercessory team. The threat of martyrdom was in the air. All I could hear in my heart and spirit was, "*To live is Christ, and to die is gain*" (Philippians 1:21).

Myles had to come to peace with the idea that if he went to the meeting, he might die. He had to come to peace that our two sons and I would be taken care of by God. He felt strongly that he couldn't shrink back in fear but that he needed to do his job, press in, and go to the meetings. We were excited about others around the world hearing about the love of God and the power of His forgiveness.

During the meeting, many came to faith in the midst of a violent assault. Rocks were thrown, gunfire was heard, and the service was unraveling. Miraculously, each rock just missed Myles. He later recounted that although he was there on the ground in a support role, it was important to go up on the platform and stand with the main minister, the true object of the ire of the agitators. He told me he thought, "If they are going to kill Roger, I should be with him." In that moment he was overcome by what felt like God wrapping fire around his body with warmth and deep peace. He saw the reality of death as expressed in the questions, *"O Death, where is your sting? O Hades, where is your victory?"* (1 Corinthians 15:55). He saw that he could trust God with his life … and death.

By the grace of God, they finished the meetings and Myles returned home to us safe and sound.

While I was on my bathroom floor singing aloud the Scripture, *"To live is Christ, and to die is gain,"* Myles was walking through that same experience, and learning that choosing Messiah is the most important thing of all. We had a connection greater than cell phones—an instant connection; it is the connection of spirit that is not limited by time or space. It moves across continents. Even though we are in geographically different places, we can still be one and know what is going on through the Holy Spirit.

Giving and receiving forgiveness is the foundation of healing every relationship. However, there are core issues that may need more attention if your marriage is going to withstand the inevitable storms. You should not be surprised that cracks in your foundation (like pornography, drugs and alcohol, mental and physical health issues, unmanaged anger, and previous unhealed traumatic violation) can tear a marriage to shreds if left unchecked. Nothing hurts a couple more than when one or both partners are in serious internal or external pain. These issues may need intensive counseling, the help of a supportive community, and a lot of humility to make it through to the finish line of freedom.

Whatever issues confront you, seek help as soon as possible. There is wisdom "*in the multitude of counselors*" (Proverbs 15:22). This also means that if you've been struggling with an issue for twenty-five years, and you are finally thinking about getting around to counseling, do it! Don't miss the moment. There is no problem too large for God to heal. He wants to intervene in your life. You have to work with Him. Acknowledge where you went wrong. Then, invite the Holy Spirit into your situation and welcome His correction, counsel, and healing. Finally, practice right behavior and responses. With God, all things are possible.

Jack and Dianne's Story

Jack and Dianne looked like the perfect couple. He was handsome, muscular, and blonde. She was dark and beautiful. They sang together with fervency, and an angelic presence would come when they worshiped together. You could say they were born to worship. They had been married eight years when they came to my office. She was considering divorce because he had had an affair.

Amidst the devastation, I prayed to God for guidance on how to help them. I knew that the traditional methodologies would not work. They had had so much expectation and religious background that, without God's intervention, they would most likely divorce.

We began the process with the retelling of their painful story. As we all wept together, you could feel the Lord's grief. Remarkably so, there was no anger or sense of condemnation. What we felt was grief, as if a precious light had almost gone out.

I questioned them about the steps that led up to the infidelity. They spoke about growing increasingly indifferent and cool towards each other, with the frustrations of his employment and their ministry life. I could see the heavy weight of trying to raise a family with little money and to fulfill the call to the ministry.

We reviewed the circumstances around their marriage, and discovered that they had engaged in pre-marital sex before their wedding. To a modern ear, this may sound antiquated and naïve, but for Jack and Dianne, the trespass of the moral foundation of their lives had created a crack in the foundation of their marriage.

I asked, "Did you ever repent?"

They looked at each other and looked at me. We sat in silence.

Jack spoke up, "Well, not formally, we just sort of acknowledged that it was wrong; then we got married." Dianne nodded in agreement.

The presence of the Lord was strong in the room, and I said, "Let's do it now!" And before my eyes, they got on their knees and repented for an event that took place eight years earlier but had now been brought into the open before God and man. The icy wall of failure and indifference broke between them as they wept their way to forgiveness and unity again. She forgave him, they forgave each other, and most importantly they experienced the forgiveness of God. They blessed one another in their hearts for the first time in many years.

> *Every Friday the man blesses his wife as a virtuous woman whose price is "far above rubies."*

Now was the time to kick the blessing meter up a notch. The foundation was being rebuilt and I wanted to introduce them to a Hebrew life custom that regularly reinforces a strong base for life. The Hebrew Shabbat begins at sundown on Friday evening and ends when the first three stars appear in the Saturday evening sky. Through the ceremonial Shabbat meal service, Jewish husbands read Proverbs 31:10–31 over their wives. Every Friday the man reinforces and blesses his wife as a virtuous woman whose price is *"far above rubies."*

The wife, not to be outdone, reads Psalm 1 over her husband and affirms that *"Blessed is the man who walks not in the counsel of the ungodly."* She reads through the short psalm to tell him what a blessing it is for her to be married to a man who is seeking God and whose life will be made whole and strengthened by that seeking.

The Berachah

The *berachah*, or blessing, means "drawing down" in Hebrew.[35]

Everything good comes from above. When we bless, we draw down health, joy, peace, and favor from heaven into the physical world. We speak what is good into existence. When we bless, we connect to God's spirit. Most relational problems we experience in life point to a disconnection from Yeshua. When we bless Him, others, and ourselves, we open the door for reconnection, healing, and restoration.

With that in mind, I instructed Jack and Dianne to consciously and intentionally build each other up by blessing one another and creating an atmosphere of unity. They began to rebuild on a foundation that was solid, a foundation that was built on the chief cornerstone, Yeshua.

To this day, Jack daily speaks to Dianne about her beauty, her strength, her wisdom, and her loveliness. Dianne speaks to Jack of her respect and her desire for him to prosper. They love each other deeply. Divorce is no longer a word in their vocabulary. Their future is bright with promise.

Ruthie's Story

As part of our first pastor's missionary team, I was sent ahead with a teammate to Baroda in Northern India, to gather church support for the upcoming celebration of Yeshua. We would enter a third-world city and gather leaders across denominational lines in anticipation of open-air healing services and daytime training schools for pastors.

On one occasion, we were assigned to a certain region in northern India where there was great resistance to the Gospel.

Several days into our trip, my traveling buddy, a Colorado cowboy, and I were called by one of the key leaders, a nurse, to pray for a troubled young woman named Ruthie, who was staying at her house. We had no idea what to expect as we entered her home.

When we stepped into the kitchen, we saw a dark figure— the young woman—at the other end of the house. Then we heard the most blood-curdling scream that either of us had ever encountered. My friend turned to me like Butch Cassidy turned to the Sundance Kid and said quietly, "You've done this before, right?"

I instantly understood that he had zero confidence in our ability to deliver this young woman from her oppression. For the next three hours, we prayed, cajoled, rebuked, and counseled our new young friend.

Eventually, she prayed the prayer of salvation and seemed to receive the forgiveness of Yeshua and to forgive those who had wronged her. Obviously exhausted, she collapsed, and we crawled back to our hotel for the night.

As I sat in the hotel room, I thought about our time with Ruthie. What had happened to this girl? I had never met anyone so wildly tormented.

In consecutive sentences, God told me she had been sold by her family into prostitution and was put on the street in a major city where she was violated repeatedly. I wrote down everything He told me on a small slip of paper, folded it, and slipped it into my pocket.

The following day we were on the prayer campaign grounds

preparing for our arriving pastor. My friend and I were finishing the details on the sound system and delegating operational instructions to the gathered leaders. Towards the middle of the day our nurse friend arrived with a beautiful young woman next to her—it was Ruthie. Ruthie smiled at my friend and me, tilting her head side to side in typical Indian fashion, and said sweetly, "Please pray for me always." She was peaceful and rational. We were amazed.

Over the course of the afternoon, I came across the nurse and slipped the list out of my pocket and into her hand. As she read over the list, her jaw dropped. God had revealed exactly what had happened to Ruthie.

Approximately one year later, we were setting up a meeting in another city in Northern India when Ruthie appeared. She was in nursing school and she smiled and said again, "Pray for me always."

Ruthie's story is a lesson to not discount that we are spiritual beings. We are vulnerable to intrusion from the spiritual realm if there are open doors in our life from trauma, abuse, and lack of forgiveness.

There is an unseen realm of spiritual life in which war between good and evil takes place. In Ruthie's case, the betrayal, rape, and forced prostitution were so traumatizing, a door had been opened to the demonic realm. To keep that door shut, Ruthie chose to forgive her parents and all those who had hurt her. Forgiveness was the key to her healing and her freedom. Her encounter with the forgiveness of Yeshua softened her heart and gave her the power to forgive those who had destroyed her life.

Sometimes psychological counseling is inadequate to begin the process of freedom. More often special prayer is required. This may be controversial to some, but in my own experience, prayer has proven to be the ultimate weapon to shut the doors against the power of darkness.

We are designed to be in relationship with God and we are created to love Him, which is how we are structured in spirit, soul, and body. If we are not filled with God, we will learn to crave other things. God has immense respect for His creation. He created us as intelligent beings with the power to choose.[36] What makes love real is our ability to choose. With that in mind, if you are choosing not to be filled with the Holy Spirit, you will choose to fill up with something else, possibly something unhealthy and destructive such as pornography, drugs, obsessive video gaming, or compulsive exercising—the list is endless. Regardless, anything that tries to fill a hole reserved for God and God alone will serve as an opening for the enemy to come in and destroy your life.

Even if a couple stays married, when one of the two habitually engages in destructive behavior, both suffer. Remember, you now have one foot. Those who are addicted live with shame, guilt, condemnation, and a sense of powerlessness. Their spouses feel betrayed, confused, and angry. These feelings are not conducive to unity and love in marriage.

In my early years of ministry, my friend Jim M. and I developed a 12-step-type program called "Trust and Triumph" for recovery from addictions. The name was based on two verses from the

Bible, Proverbs 3:5, *"Trust in the LORD with all of your heart, and lean not on your own understanding,"* and 2 Corinthians 2:14, *"Thanks be to God who always leads us in triumph in Christ."*

Our goal was to make the program available to those coming through the legal system that had been court remanded to 12-step programs. We hesitantly approached the court probation department at the civic center of our county—a large office populated by fifteen to twenty probation officers and their leaders.

"Why should we allow two church guys to work with alcoholics and junkies transitioning from jail back into life?" they asked. We read between the lines that they also questioned our ability to keep from getting hustled or manipulated by the same characters in the process.

Jim and I knowingly glanced at one another. We were more prepared to work with addicts than most. Jim had grown up on the streets of Brooklyn where he was a member of a street gang. He had a beautifully broken nose from an encounter with "six pairs of boots." Now clean and sober, and born again in Yeshua, his desire was to serve others.

I then regaled them with my elaborate journey from darkness to light. They listened patiently and unanimously granted us permission to be a court-sanctioned "step" meeting for those required by the courts to attend a recovery program.

Over time, our program was incorporated into our church. The program was then exported to local churches. Eventually "Trust and Triumph" made its way to a church plant in Siberia, where many people were addicted to vodka and/or heroin.

That was over twenty years ago.

At the time of writing this book, a report has just come from Russia about the overwhelming growth of that church plant and its satellites. Many of the church's leaders are the children of former jailbirds and addicts who were set free through "Trust and Triumph." The young pastor who brought this recent report informed me that even in Western Russia, the church leaders are Siberians. The seeds planted years ago to set addicts free paved the way for the current church growth in Russia today. Who knew?

Better Together

God created us to walk this out together. Not too long ago I was prescribed pain medication, and more pain medication, and more pain medication, for an old knee injury, which led to a total knee replacement. Finally, an Israeli doctor told me I was being poisoned and would die if I did not get off the opioids. I stopped taking them while at Auschwitz filming our next TV series. I had become dependent on them. Katharine and Yeshua, along with doctors, walked me through the recovery. The process was difficult, but Katharine and I were drawn together in a whole new way.

My hurt hurts her, too.

We are one. We go through things together. My hurt hurts her, too, and she is determined that we get better together. We are determined to bless one another every single day.

I've seen couples too scared to look at pain, sexuality, or their pasts honestly with each other or with a counselor. They choose to become roommates in marriage in lieu of receiving healing. They serve in a church, go to work, raise their kids, but tragically cannot face their sin or their shame with their spouse. Some call it quits and split up. Others miraculously take to heart what God is doing and allow God to work.

If you seek healing together, and if you can give and receive forgiveness, you and your spouse can face anything that comes your way. You will move into a Holy Spirit-inspired communion by walking *through* the offense, rather than packing the offense away where it might leap out later, causing more severe damage. However, this takes a lot of courage.

Forward Thinking

If you are always looking in the rearview mirror as you drive you are going to crash your car. If you want to move forward in your relationships, you need to look where you are going. Looking backward is a recipe for disaster. This is a main weakness in Freud's work. You can't keep looking backward and make forward progress. Sure, it is helpful to glance in the rearview mirror every once in a while, but our primary focus must be on the now and on the future.

Recovery and restoration is essentially 75 percent building a new narrative, and 25 percent problem solving. This is good news for couples that tend toward scab removing and stone overturning. The best work is done in the present, not the past: "*Now faith is the substance of things hoped for, the evidence of things not seen"*(Hebrews 11:1).

The past informs the present but does not predict the future. This also affirms the inestimable power of forgiveness! Every morning provides a fresh start.

So what does it mean to move forward?

The most important way to generate forward energy and momentum is to speak blessing over your spouse and speak gratitude to God. This often takes an act of the will. You speak out blessings over your spouse even if you don't feel like it. When you do, the atmosphere in the room will change. I think this is connected to the living power of God's Word, and that God inhabits the praises of His people (Psalm 22:3). When you are actively blessing others, you are blessing God.

Your spouse is a prime example of His handiwork. Your spouse is a blessed creature for whom Yeshua died and was resurrected. So when you bless this one, you are praising Him and His mighty works. Like Jack and Dianne, your marriage can be healed by blessing. Blessing works miracles.

If we focus on the bright side, we will succeed in our marriage, which means to verbalize and emphasize that which is of the Messiah. *"Whatever things are pure, whatever things are lovely, whatever things are of good report, . . . meditate on these things"* (Philippians 4:8). Emphasize what God is doing now. Focus on that which God is emphasizing in His loving response to us.

Ideally, this includes things that you are grateful for about your spouse. But some days, you are not in that space. My wife figured out that if you just start blessing in a general way, like, "I am grateful that I am breathing," and then work your way in, you will find things you are grateful for about your spouse even when things are pretty tense.

Try this at home:

Katharine and I have had our fair share of pressing the reset button. When we say that we forgive one another, we are done. We start over. If you can forgive, you can start over. If destructive behavior is blowing up your marriage or your life, you need intensive detoxing. One part of the battle is facing spiritual and emotional isolation from God, your spouse, and community. If you are not filled with the Holy Spirit, you will look for something else to fill your need. I purposefully remain accountable to the men around me. Do not go through life alone. God designed us to live in a community. He made us to live connected to one another.

Whenever you realize that you've hurt your spouse, go to them quickly and clean it up. If you don't know how, go to someone older and wiser and ask that person to help you clean it up. Get the help and prayer you need to be set free.

Every day, once a day, practice blessing your spouse. This means making a positive verbal statement of goodwill, faith, hope, and love. Develop the habit of drawing on the source of love and expressing His faith, hope, and love for your spouse. Read Proverbs 31:10 and following, along with Psalm 1, over one another. Let the Word of God penetrate your hearts and elevate the conversation and lifestyle you share. If you do this every day for a month or so, you will develop a lifelong practice of blessing one another. You will prosper. "You could do worse," as my grandmother might say.

Take a moment to ask what God may be asking you to face as a couple. Choose connection over disconnection, repentance over pride, and forgiveness over offense. Choose life. You can reclaim what the enemy sought to steal. Be willing to bring courage, persistence, and tenacity to face your issues head-on with the Holy Spirit. ❖

Chapter 10

HOW TO FIGHT FAIR

Tongue-Tied

One defining gift from God differentiates human beings from animals: the ability to speak. Genesis describes Adam as a living soul, *nefesh chaya*. Hebrew scholars interpret this term as "speaking spirit."[37] When we speak, much is at stake. Good speech supports our special status as human beings.[38]

Your words count. *"Death and life are in the power of the tongue"* (Proverbs 18:21). Either your conversation is infused with the Holy Spirit from above, and *"is first pure, then peaceable, gentle, willing to yield, full of mercy and good fruits, without partiality and without hypocrisy,"* or it *"does not descend from above, but is earthly, sensual, demonic. For where envy and self-seeking exist, confusion and every evil thing are there"* (James 3:17, 15–16).

Since God created the world through His Word, we can co-create and positively affect the world around us with a spoken blessing, or we can destroy it with a curse.

All your thoughts and feelings are not from God. This means that not everything I think or feel should or needs to be verbalized. Proverbs says that *"a fool vents all his feelings"* (Proverbs 29:11). A downside of being part of the Woodstock generation is that we learned to "shoot from the lip," say what you feel—just go with it. What a mess we made! It takes a lot more time to clean up a mess than to make one. Research shows it takes five affirmations to counteract one criticism.[39]

The enemy of your soul is named *"the prince of the power of the air"* (Ephesians 2:2). He might also be called the prince of the power of the airwaves because of his ability to distort our communication. I've seen this many times in counseling sessions in my office. An angry husband and wife explain their conflict. When everything is said and done, it turns out they are angry about different things! Invariably miscommunication causes misunderstanding, which causes unforgiving offense.

Katharine's Perspective: Spirit of Seduction

In ministry, you need to know that you have an enemy and that people, through their weaknesses, will try to destroy what God has brought together. Early in our marriage, Myles was counseling at the church, and there was a lady there that was jealous of our relationship. She wanted to seduce Myles away from me. I was sitting in the office when the woman came in dressed exactly as I had been the night before! The Holy Spirit quickened me to what was going on, and I warned Myles. When we move in the Spirit we can avoid the pitfalls that the enemy of our soul and our vulnerable natural life places before us. We can take a stand by speaking up to one another and speaking forth God's truth in affirmation of our marriages.

Lashon HaTov

Lashon HaTov is the Sabbath tradition of right speech. For twenty-four hours you strive to refrain from saying anything negative, sarcastic, demeaning, insulting, or critical. But it goes beyond this. The practice of *Lashon HaTov* involves speaking the positive, the blessing, the encouraging, the uplifting.[40] *Lashon HaTov* releases a miraculous power to change individuals. For example it has been demonstrated that praise empowers people to let go of the negative aspects of their character and reach their full potential, as evidenced by Lena Rustin's groundbreaking work with children suffering from stammering disorders. By teaching families how to foster a safe, encouraging environment, these children gain the ability to speak without stammering.[41]

If right speech has the power to heal as proven by empirical evidence, what does negative speech do? Specifically, what do negative speech, behavior, and attitudes do to your marriage? Let's consider anger for a moment.

There are lots of things that make us angry. No surprise there. Odds are, you have been mad at your spouse. Maybe it was merited. Perhaps you handled it well. Maybe you didn't, and you left behind a wake of devastation. Maybe you bury your anger and deny that anything upsets you. In and of itself, anger is not a bad thing. But, if mismanaged, anger can quickly become sin.

> *For all the law is fulfilled in one word, even in this: "You shall love your neighbor as yourself." But if you bite and devour one another, beware lest you be consumed by one another! I say then: Walk in the Spirit, and you shall not fulfill the lust of the flesh."* (Galatians 5:14–16)

Don't ignore anger. Don't bury it or pretend that it is not there. Don't think you shouldn't be angry. Be honest with yourself. Call it what it is. If you are angry, say so. Don't use the words *frustrated, miffed, displeased, bothered,* or *annoyed.* The first step in processing anger is honest recognition and a conscious acknowledgment that uncontrolled anger will divide you from your spouse.

Anger often flares when you feel out of control, and when you ignore the issue, the problem doesn't vaporize. The issue goes somewhere inside of you where it sits and festers. You can't pretend it is not happening. You know this is true, because the next time an event triggers anger, your response rises disproportionately higher. Why? Unresolved anger from the past informs your present. What you have not dealt with will always return to bite you in the back. If you are flipping out over the way your husband loads the dishwasher,

Unresolved anger from the past informs your present.

odds are you are actually mad at something else, something from "way back when." Maybe you never forgave your mom for her unrealistic standards in the kitchen. Maybe you need to face your control issues. Taking the courage to identify what you are actually mad about may save you years of pain.

God gives physical cues to help us quickly become aware of anger-induced adrenaline overflow. You can recognize the true issues by a tight throat, sweaty palms, reddened face and neck, a knot in your gut, and muscle tension. Don't ignore these signs. If you do, you risk exploding inappropriately at some unspecified time in the future. Over the long haul, you risk developing serious emotional and physical illnesses. By noticing the physical cues that precede anger, we can stop anger in its tracks before it spirals into sin.

The apostle James wrote, *"My beloved brethren, let every man be swift to hear, slow to speak, slow to wrath"* (James 1:19). Monitor your anger levels to develop self-awareness and self-control. Don't push your spouse's buttons, and learn how to not let your spouse press yours. Instead, recognize the physical cues of anger and practice responding well.

So what do you do when tension rises? First, acknowledge that anger is a God-given emotion. Constructive, positive anger fuels problem solving and healthy communication, which can inspire a culture to change for the better; think of the civil rights movement or the abolition of slavery.[42] However, misused anger creates condemnation and chaos and is fodder to fuel domestic violence, which opens the door to the enemy. We need to push back against the enemy and acknowledge anger for what it is. Then we need to deal with whatever real issues are at stake.

When I completed my Master's Degree in Marriage and Family Therapy, I had to complete three thousand hours of internship counseling. A local county recruited me, even though I was an intern, to manage domestic violence cases. Fresh out of graduate school, I was unprepared for the intensity of these cases and quickly realized I had jumped into a trial by fire.

My clients were two-time losers; therefore, if their wife beating didn't stop, they would spend the rest of their lives in prison. There was strong motivation to change, but little power to stop the pattern. They found themselves trapped in a vicious cycle of anger and abuse. I had never been exposed to this dimension of reparative work dealing with violence. Such abusive actions hadn't been emphasized in my graduate studies, and I had no tools to help them. So, I did what I knew how to do. I led them to Yeshua, the Ultimate Counselor. As my clients became filled with the Holy Spirit, they began to recognize that a power greater than themselves was necessary and available to implement what they were learning in my court-mandated class, "How to Stop the Violence Now!"

The first step this class taught was to take a time-out before anger escalated out of control. While this tool was especially important for my clients to learn, such a vital skill is equally necessary for anyone who wants to act righteously in the midst of stress. The person can begin by saying, "I am starting to feel angry and I need a time out."

What does that do? It takes the other person off the hook and puts you on the cross. No matter what they did to you, by using this tool, you're making a covenant that "what you do to me doesn't matter. What matters is that before God, I am committing to you to deal with my anger."

Yeshua set a standard for us forever that we have the power to deal with our anger through the Holy Spirit and not damage our spouse (or anyone else), despite what they have done to us. Remember His words on the cross, "*Father, forgive them, for they do not know what they do*" (Luke 23:34).

The next step is to leave the place you are at for an hour. You don't go drink, you don't drive, and you don't use drugs. You do something physical: walk, run, swim—just get up and move. Return after an hour and check in with the person who made you angry. Try to discuss the issue and resolve the problem then and there.

While walking, if you find yourself rehearsing how you were "done wrong" by the other person, say to yourself, "I am beginning to feel angry, and I need a time out." Pray that the Holy Spirit will help you, and believe in a positive outcome.

In fancy terms, this is cognitive behavioral transformative therapy. In spiritual terms, you are renewing your mind. This simple exercise gives you a chance to change your thoughts and feelings in order to communicate maturely with your spouse. Adults talk things out, toddlers and teenagers act things out.

This process kept my first clients out of jail. How much more efficient will it be if you are not given to violent anger as they were, but if you are just committing to your spouse to bring a more holy expression of anger and to communicate like an adult?

There are legitimate ways to express and deal with anger so that you can *"be angry, and do not sin"* (Ephesians 4:26). Criticism, showing contempt, defensiveness, and stonewalling are evil ways of dealing with anger. They are sinful and they will destroy your marriage or friendships.

How do you handle an angry spouse? Katharine often reminds me that *"a soft answer turns away wrath"* (Proverbs 15:1). We can control our speech. You know how I know that? Because you can be throwing furniture and breaking dishes on the kitchen floor, and if the pastor calls, you'll stop your tantrum on a dime and say, "Hello, Pastor" very nicely. Why not try treating our spouse as well as we would a stranger or the pastor?

Tell Me, What'd I Say?

For Katharine and me, the goal was to create an environment—a home—filled with shalom/peace. To do that, we needed to learn to communicate properly. Couples generally have a circle of messages between them. At any point in the circle, the enemy can intervene and twist both the saying and hearing of our words to cause confusion and strife. The circle is: what you mean to say, what you say, what the other person hears, what the other person thinks they hear, what the other person says about what you said, what you think about what the other person says you said and so on.

Through experience and observation, we recognized that

when we used loaded terms like "you always" or "you never," the hearer felt attacked. The constructive alternative to making blanket accusations to your spouse is to use "I statements," which typically include, "I think, I feel, I want, I need, I would like, I love...." So next time, instead of spouting out, "You always are late!" try, "I feel anxious when we are late. Can we try leaving earlier next time?"

This sounds counterintuitive but is actually a *selfless* way of communicating. This is not egocentric and liberates the other person because you are not accusing and judging them by telling them *who they are*. The other person has some breathing room.

This sounds counterintuitive but is actually a selfless way of communicating.

We also began to "check it out." Some call this the Burger King method, when you go to the drive-through and say, "I want the Whopper with cheese, the medium fries, and the drink." Then the person at the microphone *checks it out*: "Did I hear you say you want the Whopper with cheese, the medium fries, and the drink?" An interaction has just taken place that defines what you said and ensures you are getting across to the other person the message you want to communicate. Practice this by saying something and have your spouse *check it out* with you. For example, "I hear you saying that you feel anxious when I lag behind. Is that right?"

These two techniques transform marriages by rewriting the rules of engagement—that is, how you and your spouse engage one another. I've seen people who continually miss each other and miscommunicate suffer because they don't use "I statements" or *check it out* to make sure they are understood. On the other hand, some couples are transformed by incorporating these keys into their communication. It is amazing how clarity defuses otherwise potentially incendiary situations.

Try this at home: ▬▬▬▬▬▬▬▬▬▬▬▬▬▬▬▬▬▬▬

As a couple, recognize your common enemy. He wants to tear down your household, split you up, and destroy what God is building. Remember, you have an enemy, but it is not your spouse. Put down this book, look at your spouse, and say, "You are not my enemy!"

Guarding the content and quality of your speech could be the most important step you take to strengthen and protect your marriage.

Take a practice time-out when you are not angry with your spouse. This will give you brain and muscle memory so that in times of anger you will know what to do in order to not escalate the battle.

Practice "I statements" and *checking it out* with each other. Simplify your communication. Don't presume to know what your spouse is thinking or feeling. Simply state what you are feeling or thinking and make sure you understand what they are saying by repeating their thoughts back to them.

Finally, practice *Lashon HaTov* all week long. Apologize and ask for forgiveness if you make a mistake and become negative. Strive to not let unholy speech leave your mouth. Always communicate with love, respect, and gentleness. If you do that, your life will be filled with shalom, *"the peace of God, which surpasses all understanding"* (Philippians 4:7). ❖

Chapter 11

MEET ME IN THE MIDDLE

The Difference Between Men and Women

Katharine and I could not be more different. I am Jewish. She is Gentile. I am enough older than her to be from a different generation, and I come from a New York wisecracking, sarcastic, negative family. Katharine's family was always focused on image and wealth. She likes slapstick and physical comedy, while I relish word play, amusing banter, and historical references. Believe me, we brought deep cultural differences into our marriage that needed major navigating. We were not always on the same page. For our marriage to thrive and survive, we had to learn to believe for the best in each other.

One difference in particular trumped the others and explained the source of many of our disagreements and misunderstandings. I am a man, and Katharine is a woman. A big factor in staying in love relates to a basic understanding that men and women are not the same.

Gender differences are a basic source of communication problems. You and your spouse are *really* different from one another. You have probably figured that out by now, haven't you? We spend an enormous amount of energy trying to make the other over in our image. That's not the way God designed us to be, and our attempts are doomed to fail. Praise the Lord! If husband and wife were identical in every respect, marriage would be dreadfully dull.

I must often counsel couples and say, "Forget it. You are not going to make him think and act like a woman, and you are not going to make her think and act like a man." Women are often surprised *Your husband can never and will never be your girlfriend.* because they want their husband to act like a girlfriend. Your husband can never and will never be your girlfriend. God designed you differently on purpose. Wives need their husbands' strength and God-given authority.

Men are often surprised that their wives don't like to be treated like one of the guys. She needs gentleness, kindness, and patience. Husbands need their wives' emotional intelligence and ability to sense danger to avoid pitfalls, false friends, and traps.

Genesis describes Eve's creation with the word *vayiven*, which comes from the root word *binah*, meaning "insight." The Talmud explains that this word was used to show that women were created with an extra dose of wisdom and intuition.[43] It suggests that women have a unique, God-given ability to understand a situation from the inside out, in great detail. This sort of intellect lends itself to higher internal emotional intelligence. Men, in contrast, are described with the word *da'at*. *Da'at* implies wisdom and understanding from the outside in. Men have the ability to see the big picture, with the sort of intellect associated more with facts, figures, and logic. The husband's strength is external.[44]

When these differences blend to strengthen one another—when a man and woman pool their unique giftings and understanding—they become an unabridged version of what God created them to be. We cannot and should not ask each other to be more like our gender. Let men be men and women be women.

The Science

The Torah gives excellent insight into gender differences. Yes, feminine-masculine differences are not just stereotypes. We are not made from cookie cutters; we are uniquely fashioned and endowed with specific gifts and callings. Modern neurology (brain science) and psychology confirm what we understand naturally, and what the Bible says: the differences between men and women are not limited to biological differences.

Did you know that there is a 2 percent difference between men's and women's brains? That 2 percent of grey matter matters! Men have six times more gray matter than women and women have ten times more white matter than men. In laymen's terms, men can focus on an isolated big picture. Women have the ability to see connections and details linking information from a variety of sources.[45]

While generally men and women can perform the same functions, they tend not to perform them in the same way. God designed the differences this way for our benefit. Learning and understanding your spouse's unique gender attributes, and selflessly serving one another in love, enhances intelligence and mental health.[46]

Most married couples have experienced the following scenario: The classic story is that *he* takes the phone call that cousin Teri had a baby. *She* comes home and asks if they heard from cousin Teri. Here is the conversation that follows:

"Yeah, ummmm, she had a baby!"

"Well, what was it?"

"Well, it was a baby."

"Was it a boy or a girl?"

"I don't know; it was a baby."

"How long was it?"

"I don't know!"

Now, if *she* had picked up the call, she would know that the baby was a girl named Elizabeth, seventeen inches long and weighing six pounds eight ounces. She would also know who was at the delivery and what happened afterward and all the important details.

Men's brains have compartments in them that don't touch each other, and so they tend to do one thing at a time. We men are more linear, more sequential. We complete one task, then move on to the next. We are serial doers. A man stops, thinks, and then recharges. He can take a thought and store it somewhere for later. Women, with more white matter, link a thought to another thought, and another thought after that, and on and on.[47] The point here is not that these differences are set in stone, but that they give us the opportunity to show love and mercy to those who process differently.

The Nothing Box

Men have a special refuge in their brain that Pastor Mark Gungor, among others, calls the *nothing box*. This is the place men go when they are stressed, or processing heavily. No one gets in this box, except maybe his dog. Ladies, you are not allowed in the box.[48] The *nothing box* enhances a man's serial ability to do things well. For example, we can golf well, or fish, or be a chef, a brain surgeon, plumber, or rocket scientist, but we do it sequentially—one task at a time. The *nothing box* provides down time that recharges men for the next task on the list. Take note, though, that because it is off limits to women, it can challenge communication in a marriage.

When men are stressed, they want to retreat into the *nothing box*. They don't want to talk about what happened. I go through seasons where my guitar is my *nothing box* du jour. I play between counseling sessions and sometimes at home when things are on my mind, or I am feeling stressed. This is how I relieve stress, process, and relax.

By contrast, when most women experience stress, they want to talk about it. And they will keep talking about it. They will walk for ten miles with five friends and talk about it and address it from every possible angle. They will run through every possible outcome, not just once but multiple times.

Please note, not every woman does this out loud. Some women need a *nothing box* of their own before they can process through something with friends or with you. Everyone is unique and needs to be in tune with how they handle recharging, processing, and decision making.

For men to hear their wives, they must stop the one thing they are doing, focus, and listen. A man can only be in one box at a time. If he is in the newspaper or TV box, he cannot be in the listening box. At the same time, women, who seem to do a hundred things at once, need to stop everything they are doing and talk directly to the man. She has to connect with her husband and say things more than once. Why does she have to say things more than once? Because men process information differently.

For men to hear their wives, they must stop the one thing they are doing, focus and listen.

A familiar tale involves the wife communicating from another area code—like the upstairs master bathroom—to her husband downstairs in the family room. She is trying to impart important information about a place he needs to be a week from Monday at 6:00 p.m. Her voice can barely be made out over the running water of the shower. When he misses the appointment a week later, she says, "You don't listen to me!" She just doesn't understand why he never listens and follows through. I will tell you why. She needs to stop and talk to him in the same area code if she wants to communicate with her man.

And men, you need to stop and listen. It will be good for you. She will help you get to where you need to be next Monday at 6:00 p.m. because it is highly possible you forgot in a haze of detail.

That Time of Day

Picture the following: Marvin and Shelley have been married for fifteen years. Their eldest daughter, Jenny, fell into some serious trouble at school. Both Marvin and Shelley are stressed out and worried. Neither knows what to do. Marvin returns home from work and retreats into his stereo system. Shelley pounces on him and begins to release a long, loud, intense stream of consciousness speech covering every single one of her worries over their daughter's future. Marvin is silent until he cuts his wife off with a blunt solution of how to handle Jenny once she returns from school. This causes Shelley to explode even more. How can Marvin say that? Doesn't he see all the angles? Marvin now feels defensive and angry. They spiral apart and out of control. And this is the fifth time they fought all evening in the last two weeks.

What's wrong?

God wants us to communicate with one another. Knowing when, what, and how to communicate is a big part of doing it well. Between 4:00 and 8:00 every evening, according to Dr. Caroline Leaf, your brain processes the day as it starts to prepare for bed.[49] Women work out their solutions while they are talking. When men finally do speak, they express the solutions they already worked out inside their heads.[50] Many women cannot understand why their husbands don't want to talk, while husbands get equally annoyed at their wives for invading their quiet time. The thing is, both men and women need this time to process before they can have a real conversation. If we impose our different ways of processing on one another, there will be friction.[51]

Consider talking through the big stuff *after* dinner, once your brains have finished processing the day. At this point, the man will be prepared to debrief, and the woman will have organized her thoughts into something more succinct and clear.[52]

When I speak publicly, Katharine always tells me what a great job I did, how inspirational I was, what a great teacher I am, first. She will tell me how I could have improved later. After we have appeared on TV, we do the same with each other. If she has an idea for how to improve something, she always shares it gently and kindly, normally the next day. Because I know she respects me, I can hear and incorporate her ideas, which have greatly improved my public speaking abilities through the years.

Katharine's Perspective:
Knowing When to Hold My Tongue

After people preach, they are particularly vulnerable because they have just given out their best. It is important to know whether what you are saying at that moment will give life or not. For instance, there was a time when Myles was preaching and I saw how his sarcastic humor detracted from the message he was bringing, instead of enhancing it. I had learned the hard way to wait for the right time, and for the unction of the Holy Spirit, to give him input. This time, it was the following day when I was able to tell Myles that his humor might not always be the avenue that will bring people the help they need. Fortunately, shortly thereafter, the Holy Spirit spoke to him that sometimes there was a word of knowledge or encouragement that He (the Spirit) wanted to bring that was hampered by Myles' quick-witted sarcasm.

I know from counseling hundreds of couples that many women desire to process verbally with their husbands and are not really interested in an immediate solution. I've also learned that men sometimes need just to rant to get something out of their system. At times like these, they don't want their wives' input immediately. It's a good practice to tell your spouse not to cut you off or jump in with an idea or solution when you are verbally processing or ranting. You need to allow one another to finish getting something out of your system before processing through a solution together. Over time, Katharine and I have come to a place where we laugh when I ask her, "Is this something you want me to fix, or is this something you want me just to listen to?"

Try this at home: ▬▬▬▬▬▬▬▬▬▬▬▬▬▬▬▬▬▬▬▬▬▬▬▬▬

Make a list of how you and your spouse differ. In what ways can these differences strengthen you and help fill in gaps? In what ways can you be more sensitive to your spouse's uniqueness as a man or woman?

Practice giving your husband space.

Vice versa, guys, listen—really listen to your wife.

When you truly desire to learn about your spouse's needs and hear what he or she is trying to say, you are taking positive action to discipline your mind to react well and treat your spouse as a son or daughter of the living God. Celebrate your differences. Celebrate that you are both made in God's image. Celebrate that you are better together. ❖

Chapter 12

RULES, ROLES, RITUALS... OR RELATIONSHIP?

Remembrance and Ceremony

Only take heed to yourself, and diligently keep yourself,
lest you forget the things your eyes have seen, and lest
they depart from your heart all the days of your life. And
teach them to your children and your grandchildren.

(Deuteronomy 4:9)

Remembrance is a vital part of being a believer. We are called to remember the Sabbath and to remember the annual Passover celebration. The Feast of Trumpets, Rosh HaShanah, reminds us with each trumpet blast to remember to worship the Lord and to remind Him of His promises to us. Throughout his letters, Paul admonished the young church to remember the teachings of the apostles. And Yeshua, on the eve of His death, promised that His Holy Spirit, the Comforter, would help us remember what He taught us.

Somewhere high on the west bank of the Jordan River near Gilgal, twelve stones stand as a memorial. Joshua placed these stones to be visual reminders for all future generations of Israel to remember God's goodness for leading them to the Promised Land:

> ... that this may be a sign among you when your children
> ask in time to come, saying, "What do these stones mean
> to you?" Then you shall answer them that the waters of
> the Jordan were cut off before the ark of the covenant of
> the LORD; when it crossed over the Jordan, the waters of
> the Jordan were cut off. And these stones shall be for a
> memorial to the children of Israel forever. (Joshua 4:6–7)

Katharine and I have our memorial stones, personal stones that we return to year after year to remind our family what God has done. These stones stabilize our marriage. They retell us why we fell in love and help us to fall in love all over again.

We know a couple, another Jewish-Gentile match, who shared their first kiss on Ben Yehuda Street in Jerusalem. Now, whenever they are in Israel, they make sure to re-create the moment and take a picture under the street sign. That is a precious, simple memorial stone.

Every year on the first day of school, we photographed our boys standing next to the same tree to record their growth. We would walk as a family in the evening to the same spot, throw the football around a bit, and take the photo. It was a tradition for me to take a sip of their soda on the walk. Our boys remind us, "It's tradition, Dad!" Without the ceremonial sip of soda, the day wasn't the same.

Remembrance and ceremony connect us to the past and give us hope for the future, reminding us of who God is, what He has done, and what He will do. We worship collectively in our believing communities through remembrance. This is what we do when we gather and go through the various parts of a service.

Sometimes we miss seeing how much of Christian life is ceremonial. For example, we often repeat the same pattern in Sunday services: Greeting, Prayer, Songs, Announcements, Offering, Song, Sermon, Song, Altar Call, and Benediction. We call this "decent and in order," rather than ceremonial or ritualistic.

As believers in Yeshua, we often shy away from ritual and ceremony. What we don't realize is that tradition can open the door for hearts to receive Yeshua. We wrongly assume that all tradition is a religious trap; the exact thing Yeshua frees us from. In truth, tradition working hand in hand with the Holy Spirit has great power and can open the door for the Holy Spirit to work in powerful ways.

Katharine's Perspective: The Scrunchie

Myles and I have learned over the course of our relationship that God is concerned about every little detail in our life. There is no issue that is too small to bring before God. One weekend we were in Florida closing out Myles' mother's apartment after she passed away. We were enjoying a day in the beautiful turquoise water of south Florida. I turned to Myles and said, "What a perfect day!" The beach was white, the water warm and blue, and I had packed well. I had all the right "girl" stuff I needed with me. Well, almost all. I casually remarked, "The only thing I wish I had packed is a 'scrunchie.'" [*Guys, that's a hair-rubber-band-pull-and-tie-back thingy — Myles*] At that point, as if on command, the sparkling waves of water pushed up a black velvet scrunchie right in front of us! Now, we fully understand that others in remote parts of the world are facing existential issues of crushing weight. Still, it was such a small detail, so lovingly attended to; it gave credence to the words of Yeshua that "*all these things shall be added to you*" if you seek His kingdom (Matthew 6:33). For us, even something as mundane as a scrunchie became a memorial stone, reminding us to ask our Father for the things that we need.

Max's Story

A ninety-six-year-old Jewish man, Max, came to Beth Shalom when we used to meet in our home. He shuffled in and took his seat amidst the dozens of disciples of Yeshua and Jewish and Gentile seekers who joined with our small family to enter into the Sabbath rest. We all gathered around Katharine, who lit her match and quietly said the blessing over the lighting of the candles.

Baruch Atah Adonai, Eloheinu Melech haolam,
Asher kiddeshanu b'mitzvotav v'tzivanu l'hadlik ner shel
Shabbat.

"Blessed are You, O Lord our God, King of the universe, Who has sanctified us and commanded us to light the Sabbath candles [keep the Sabbath]." She went on to say, "As believers, we adapt this prayer to acknowledge Yeshua as *Or haOlam,* The Light of the World."

"We adapt this prayer to acknowledge Yeshua as Or haOlam, *The Light of the World."*

Hebrew days begin at sundown, so the candles are lit for the Sabbath at dusk. The tradition is to light them eighteen minutes before sunset to avoid desecrating the Sabbath through working, because according to Scripture it is a time of rest. Eighteen is a traditional number used in blessing. It is the numerical equivalent of the letters that make up the Hebrew word *chai,* which means "life." (*Chai* is not pronounced like the Indian tea; instead the "ch" is a guttural, throaty sound, like you're about to spit. As the comedian Billy Crystal said, "this is a language of coughing and spitting."[53])

The two candles also represent these verses from Torah: "*Remember the Sabbath*" (Exodus 20:8) and "*Observe the Sabbath*" (Deuteronomy 5:12). Two candles fit beautifully with the picture of the "one new man," Jew and Gentile together in Messiah. Some Jewish women light a seven-candle menorah (candelabra) to thank God for the seven days of the week. Families often light one candle for each of their children. The simple act of lighting the candles and praying a simple prayer of thanks kindles the experience of breathing together in the presence of God. This is a ritual that never grows old.

The night that Max joined our Shabbat, the presence of God was particularly tangible. Max marveled at the candle lighting when it included the presence of Yeshua. He stood weeping in my kitchen, saying, "I have not felt this way since my wife died. I have been so lonely, and I don't feel alone anymore. What is happening to me?" He was radiant with the revelation of love.

"Max," I replied with tears in my eyes, "Yeshua is the one the Gentiles call Jesus. He is saving your soul, and He will take you to heaven to be with Him."

We walked to the car at the evening's end, and as I knelt down to say goodbye, Max turned stiffly in the front seat. "I have such neck pain," Max whispered hoarsely. I told him, "The prophet Isaiah stated that Messiah would bear our sins and our sicknesses. May I pray for your neck?"

He sighed, "Why not? This is a most unusual night." God healed his neck like a father kissing his favorite son. Max died a few months later, but we know he is alive in the presence of his Messiah. He is alive in the Light.

By creating a space where Max felt safe, a Shabbat service like those he might have remembered from his Jewish upbringing, the Holy Spirit was able to touch Max's heart and heal his body supernaturally.

Finding Balance

A Methodist pastor once glowingly reported that our Shabbat services were "first-century style," with, simultaneously, people worshiping in one room, kids playing around outside, a woman getting healed in the kitchen, and a group laughing on the patio. The Shabbat celebration burst with life, energy, and freedom. We were celebrating tradition without being traditional.

There is a risk in congregations where synagogue ceremony, liturgy, and style edge out the presence of Yeshua. In our home we were never rigid about keeping kosher (Yeshua set us free. Love trumps your diet. What comes out of your mouth, not what goes in, is what matters.) When tradition suffocates the presence of God and the person of Yeshua, watch out. You are in trouble.

Max showed us that when tradition elevates Yeshua, the transformative, saving power of God is magnified. Jewish ministry is effective when the Church is involved. There is meaning and purpose in the various holidays and feasts, as well as great wisdom from God to glean, to walk in, and to align with during the festivals of the Lord. In these seasons, the Lord provides fresh starts and new seasons.

That said, Katharine and I value flexibility and seek to know what the Lord is asking us to celebrate, and what to remember, as a couple and as leaders of a congregation.

As a Jew and Gentile, we bring different traditions to the table. Every spouse, regardless of background, comes into a marriage with expectations regarding how holidays will be remembered. For a Jew and Gentile, these differences of expectation can cause a lot of problems: to celebrate Christmas or not to celebrate Christmas! If you celebrate Christmas, do you open presents in the morning or on Christmas Eve? Do you say "Jesus"? Or "Yeshua"? Should you celebrate Shabbat every week? What about all the other feasts? Do you eat bacon or not eat bacon? Do you tell the kids the Easter Bunny is a hoax? Just kidding. Regardless, these are the questions every *"one new man"* couple has asked at least once, and every married couple has asked as well.

The answers to these questions can spark disagreements and hurt feelings, or they can birth new family traditions for remembrance that are extraordinary and sweet. Neither Katharine nor I were content with the traditions we inherited. What we found in Yeshua opened the door to new life through the old.

If you are in Yeshua, you are a new creation. You have the freedom to build and celebrate, to remember, to enjoy life— however the Holy Spirit leads. For us, that meant merging Katharine's Catholic upbringing with my Jewish traditions. She embraced the High Holy Days while I learned "O Holy Night." We showed our love for one another by embracing what was different in each other. We were becoming the *"one new man."*

A Blue and White Christmas

I remember it like it was yesterday. With my heart racing and my hands frozen to the steering wheel, my rental car slowly rolled into the expansive driveway. Luxury cars silently testified to the neighborhood's status. The wiper blades swooshed back

and forth. "Swoosh, swoosh, swoosh, Jewish, Jewish, Jewish...."
Great, I'm hallucinating! Wiper blades are not anti-Semitic!

The "Christmas mansion" appeared through the trees. The culture clash was under way. I seemed to hear my grandma say, "What's a nice Jewish boy like you doing in a palace like this?" I rang the bell.

Christmas had always been an awkward time of year for me. The difference between mainstream American Christian culture and my Jewish family was most apparent in December. At best we were silent outsiders; at worst we were Christ-killers. As a teenager, many spirited religious discussions were resolved by an obligatory punch in the nose—emphasizing the superiority of Catholic doctrine over Jewish protests. Being a Jew in a Christian world can be dangerous. My peers were verifying my grandmother's message. Her history of Christianity went like this: Crusades, Inquisition, Holocaust. Two thousand years of persecution, expulsion, and execution, Christians were brutal zealots. I was wary to say the least. But now I was in love with one of them.

The door opened, and Katharine stood there smiling. In the candle-lit room, her olive skin contrasted with her white winter dress. She radiated seasonal good will with a subtle undertone of special warmth. Our chemistry was greater than the history the world had ever known. I was willing to risk overturning Grandma in her grave to marry this beauty.

On her part, Katharine had parted ways with a millionaire male model to spend time with me. She sat outside his Pacific

Heights mansion in his Ferrari, and an inner voice told her, "You will wind up divorced and unhappy if you say yes." Good news for me, but not for her parents. She had left the catch of the century to be with me: a short, older, Jewish guy who loved her. Now here I was in their house on Christmas, while back in New York City, Chanukah had begun.

We embraced and held each other close. I didn't want to let go. She was safe and warm and she knew I was dreading the encounter with her parents.

"I'm so glad you came," she whispered.

"Wouldn't miss it," I assured her. Actually, at the airport I had considered getting back on the plane and leaving town.

Her mom came prancing down the grand, gilded staircase. She was all smiles and looked like Hollywood royalty. The entrance hall was bigger than my apartment. The lights and candles everywhere reminded me of Rockefeller Center. I stumbled through a continental air kiss with Mom, which left me off balance and seemed to stretch her decorum as well. Left air, right air, forced smiles, and hand held lightly. Awkward.

"We are thrilled to have you here, Morris," her Mom said.

"It's *Myles*," her daughter corrected.

"Of course, it is, Dear. Well, I'll leave you two and attend to the appetizers. I hope you're hungry, Mor ... uh, Myles. We're having crab dip and bacon-wrapped prawns." I imagined generations of kosher-keeping ancestors fainting over in rows, like stacked slabs of pork ... um ... beef ribs.

The glow from the next room was unearthly. We entered the

living room to behold the biggest Christmas tree in domestic captivity, filling the room and touching the ceiling. I must have gasped.

"A bit much, eh?" Katharine whispered in my ear.

We hovered at the edge of the room. Brightly wrapped silver and red packages covered the floor. We could not reach the tree through the minefield of gifts.

"They're color coordinated," I muttered.

"Yes, each year we use a different theme," Katharine explained.

I felt in my pocket for the tiny box. I still had it. *What was I thinking?* My gift for Katharine was a small custom-made silver pendant with a verse from the book of Ruth written in gold. The heartfelt trinket seemed inadequate. We were worlds apart. How could we ever reconcile these differences? I sighed.

"Are you okay?" Katharine asked.

"Sure, great, never better."

Was my clenched jaw visible over my shallow breathing?

I took Katharine's hand, and the electric warmth traveled up our arms to our hearts. We smiled. I relaxed. We sat on the antique bench just inside the doorway. I reached into my pocket for her gift. My hand stuck mid-purpose, and I leaped to my feet. The Major appeared across the room.

Major Burke commanded any room he entered. People naturally stood to attention and felt compelled to salute. He was the quintessential leader: tall and athletic, patrician in appearance with graying temples, face tanned from golf, tennis, and yachting; and he loved his daughter.

"I'll meet you in the library," he called. Apparently they were used to circumnavigating the gift room.

"Yes sir," I croaked. *Oh, man, I thought, here we go. Time for inspection. Troops about face. To the library, March!*

"Hi." *Brilliant opener, Morris.*

"Hello, son. Merry Christmas."

"Happy Chanukah to you, sir."

I emphasized the guttural "*kch*" sound. *Couldn't help it, could you? Have to be the wise guy, don't you?*

The Major cleared his throat. "Yes, of course, Happy Ha-anoo-kaa," his tongue twisted as his brows furrowed and his face cramped. Katharine joined us.

"How's my favorite middle girl?" The Major lifted his daughter off the ground and hugged her tightly.

"Merry Christmas and Happy Chanukah, Daddy," Katharine said. She must have practiced the "chhh" in Chanukah. She sounded so natural, she could have been my Aunt Mildred bargaining with her butcher in Brooklyn. I was impressed again.

She could have been my Aunt Mildred bargaining with her butcher in Brooklyn.

A tinkling bell announced dinner, and we assembled in the grand dining room. A banquet table was covered in white linen, with silver settings for every culinary task. The room sparkled with enough candles to light St. Patrick's Cathedral. The meal was sumptuous. The family warily eyed me, hoping for the best. They could see how I felt about their sweet daughter. Our loving manner with each other touched them and I relaxed. *They want her to be happy.* I began to like them.

Dinner was followed by the gift-opening ritual. The opulence was overwhelming. I started to sweat. Finally, we came to the end of the packages. The room looked like a retail war zone. Red and silver paper explosions were piled three feet deep.

Katharine and I looked across the room at each other. We peered over the holiday shreds of paper shrapnel. This was our moment. We exchanged gifts and eagerly opened the cards. Our cards affirmed our love and spoke of gratitude to God for bringing us together. In them, we acknowledged our debt to Messiah Jesus. He had become the center of our hearts and was teaching us the grace of His salvation. We were enjoying the fruit of unity in the spirit. We believed the testimony of the apostle Paul. He had written to the Ephesian congregation that Jesus abolished the wall of separation between Jew and Gentile. When He died for our sins, He made us into *"one new man,"* a unified body of believers. I was free to celebrate the feasts of the Lord as a Jew, who followed Messiah. My modern day Ruth was grafted into the olive tree symbolizing the faith-filled remnant of Israel.

We read our cards aloud and explained to Katharine's parents that without Chanukah there would be no Christmas. God had preserved the family of Jews by miraculously defeating their oppressors in the century before the birth of Jesus. The sacred oil for the temple supernaturally lasted for eight days instead of one.

I opened my present. Katharine presented me with a small

---

handcrafted menorah. The Chanukah candelabrum was fashioned of silver and gold. I breathed deeply and thanked her. Tears welled in her eyes.

She opened her gift. The pendant read, *"Your people shall be my people, and your God, my God."* The words from the book of Ruth were alive. Ruth was the Gentile woman who married into the family of Israel and became King David's—and thus Jesus'—ancestor. Peace settled on us all as we sat in silence. Centuries of conflict seemed to melt away. The Major smiled and dabbed at his eye with a napkin.

"Happy Chanukah, son," he said.

"Merry Christmas, Major."

Try this at home:

Whether and how you celebrate Christmas or Chanukah, or any remembrances, is up to you and your spouse. The key concept is that as a man and woman you are linked *despite your differences.* Yeshua is the tie binding you together, guiding you as a couple through life. Through Him flows a spirit of love, forgiveness, and openness towards one another. If that means your spouse is Jewish and wants to celebrate a Seder, do so out of love! My love for Katharine made me open to celebrating Christmas. Be open to seasons changing as well. As our boys got older, for example, we phased out Christmas trees.

Little traditions have just as much power—perhaps more power—than big ones when you have children. Eating dinner several times a week as a family, asking about the highs and lows of the week, going to prayer meetings, learning how to declare God's goodness in a public setting, provided a solid foundation for our boys to grow up in a Messiah-centered environment. On a lighter note, regularly playing two-on-two (Katharine and our elder son Jonathan vs. our younger son Stephen and me) on the basketball court kept the four of us close and taught us how to work together as a team.

As a couple, try to create traditions that get you out of your daily routine. Day trips to the snow or the beach, plus an annual summer and winter vacation, work wonders. Not being surrounded by your everyday pressures will help you focus on the Lord and your spouse in a new way.

Celebrate the milestones of your relationship. Remember why you first fell in love. Tell each other what you are grateful for, and do so regularly. Savor the delicious moments of a weekly Sabbath and fill up on the joy of holidays, the fun of outings, and the quiet pleasure of simply spending time together, measuring the years and remembering the wonders of what God has done. ❖

Chapter 13

WHOLLY REST

George & Lily's Story

The first time I encountered people of faith was when I met George and Lily. George was a diminutive wizened black man from the Caribbean. The singsong lilt in his voice betrayed his island heritage. He moved to the States from Barbados as a young man and worked his way to home ownership in a small Massachusetts town near Cape Cod.

The era was the 1960s. My friends and I were in our back-to-the-land phase. We had visions of self-sufficiency and getting off the grid. We lived near George and his wife Lily, and he became my gardening mentor. I would stop by their place to cut flowers for our house. They always had plenty to share. He wasn't a rich man but lived a rich life. He and Lily grew flowers, fruit trees, and veggies, all with a grateful attitude.

On the exterior wall next to the front door, George had hung metallic letters spelling the Hebrew name, *Ebenezer*, "the Lord has been my help." He had named his home Ebenezer.

George was the real deal. "Mon, sometimes me and de old lady lay in bed and tank God for all we got—if it's raining, we got a roof—if we ain't got a loaf uh bread, we got half a loaf, yess suh."

I marveled at the oneness he and his wife shared—the deeply loving way he honored and cared for Lily. "How long you been married, George?"

"Mon, it seems like forever!" Lily smiled at me from the front porch. George winked at her.

"George, you gonna plant those sweet onions again this year?"

"I don' know, mon. This year I tink I be singin' in hebben," he grinned.

George died that winter.

I was the only white guy at George's funeral. The singing and preaching I experienced at George and Lily's black Pentecostal church were my first exposure to real Christianity. I didn't understand much, but what I heard that day impressed me with a profound sense of hope. That day I was surrounded and accepted by people who embraced a joyful expectation that reached past the grave. They spoke about George as if he were still alive in another room, but at the same time far away. It was strange and it was holy.

George and Lily shared something incredible. I had experienced it to a lesser degree growing up in a traditional Jewish home, but nothing compared to George and Lily. They shared a spiritual community. They lived together in a perpetual communion of the bread and wine of friendship around the marriage table. Their long-lasting relationship was deep and deeply infused with the presence of God. Looking back, it occurs to me that they sanctified time itself. They lived, moved, and breathed the Sabbath peace, or *Shabbat Shalom*. I couldn't grasp it completely, but I knew it was something I needed.

The Gift of the Shabbat

As a boy, I remember watching my father hold up the kiddush cup, the cup of sweet red Shabbat wine. The wine glistened at the brim with jewel-like intensity in the glow of the candles my mother had lit. My father recited the Hebrew blessing over the wine, reminding us that Shabbat is our inheritance, our special gift from God, and we are to keep it holy. He would then hold up two sweet braided challah loaves and bless them. We each broke off a chunk, dipped it in salt, and ate. Like millions of Jews the world over, we welcomed Shabbat, the "bride" of the Jewish people.

An ancient midrash teaches that all the days of the week have mates. Sunday has Monday. Tuesday has Wednesday. Thursday has Friday. But Shabbat? There is an old story that Shabbat complained to God that it too needed a spouse. God listened and gave Shabbat the Jewish people to be its companion and groom.[54]

The wine and bread, the blessings, and the songs of praise and remembrance demarcated the Shabbat from the other six days of the week. For the next twenty-four hours, we rested from our labors and spent time worshiping God, and enjoying family and friends.

God designed us. He, more than any doctor or psychologist,

knows our critical need for rest. Even He rested on the seventh day! Without rest, we burn out and stumble. Without rest, our level of work performance and the quality of our relationships dip significantly.

God gave us Shabbat in the same way He gave Eve to Adam. Shabbat is our helper. When we embrace Shabbat, when we stop and rest, when we contemplate what God has done, we gain perspective and restorative energy. We see the big picture and focus on others. We welcome the Holy Spirit into the approaching workweek, and into our relationships, through the sacrament of breaking bread, sharing wine, and entering into the holy rest of Yeshua.

Of course, without Yeshua, my childhood Sabbaths were missing something. Those Saturdays didn't fulfill my unspoken longing for true communion and rest. Steeped in ritual, I knew from an early age that there had to be more.

In particular, I've learned over the years that Shabbat is an essential key to a good marriage. The workweek for most of us is packed with stressful activity that can introduce divisive elements into marriage. Maybe one of the reasons God gave us the Sabbath is to require husbands and wives to enjoy each other, free from day-to-day distractions. Simi Lichtman, a newlywed Orthodox young woman, wisely wrote in *The Forward*:

> After a week of work and school and distraction, of television and texting and typing, Shabbat is 25 hours where it's just me and Jeremy and nothing in between us. Even if we wanted to avoid each other, all we have are

books and magazines to distract us from one another....
Life is simpler on Shabbat, and so is our relationship.
If we disagree, we have hours to talk it out, instead of
having to work our discussions around the rest of life's
demands. A day without technology has always been, for
me, a day to recharge and prepare for the coming week
while allowing the past one to wash away. Now it's a time
where my relationship can benefit, too.[55]

Followers of Yeshua are free from the myriad of hyper-
restrictive, ultra-Orthodox Shabbat rules and regulations. But
perhaps it's not a bad idea to turn off the cell phone and the Internet
for a day and reconnect with the ones you love, especially your
spouse. With that in mind, let's talk about what it means when
we celebrate Shabbat as a couple. What is the deeper meaning of
the wine and the bread that are central to the traditional Shabbat
observance? How are Shabbat and communion connected? What
does the lesson of Shabbat teach us as married couples?

The Wine and the Bread

The wine and the bread predate the Passover, the Last Supper,
and communion. When Melchizedek, the King of Salem, brings
wine and bread to Abram (Genesis 14:18–20), he blesses Abram
and the Most High God. This is the first mention of partaking of
communion in the Scriptures.

Some two thousand years later, when Yeshua initiates His New
Covenant at the Passover Seder (the Last Supper) the evening
before His crucifixion, He gives a new understanding of the

wine and bread. It seals the betrothal between Yeshua and His believers—His Bride—and it also gives us a way to experience His body and blood in remembrance of His finished work on the cross, precisely the work that enables us to rest. Freed from the necessity to work for our salvation by following all those rules that we can't keep, we have our true Shabbat Shalom as a free gift from the Sar Shalom, the Prince of Peace, the only One with authority to give us that peace. As we take the wine and bread of the New Covenant, the burden of our sin is lifted off our shoulders. This was what I was missing in the Shabbat observances of my childhood: the Shabbat perfected.

When we bless the wine during the traditional Shabbat observance, we pray:

> *Baruch Atah Adonai, Eloheinu Melech haolam,*
> *Borei p'ri hagafen.*
> Blessed are You, Lord our God, King of the universe,
> Who creates the fruit of the vine.

This is a prophetic declaration that refers to Yeshua, the Messiah, the actual "first fruit." Yeshua is the vine; we are the branches (John 15:5). Because He was tread on (like grapes crushed underfoot in the wine-making process), we receive joy, freedom, and rest.

The kiddush cup overflowing reminds us of His overflowing blessings and love. The cup overflows with His presence, healing, and joy. Whatever you fill yourself with will spill onto others— just something to consider.

Remember Psalm 23:5–6: *"You prepare a table before me in the presence of my enemies; You anoint my head with oil; my cup runs over. Surely goodness and mercy shall follow me all the days of my life; and I will dwell in the house of the* LORD *forever."*

Yeshua fills our cup with Himself. When we partake, we enter into His house. Forever. We enter into betrothal and become His figurative Bride.

In Jewish tradition, a man could ask a woman to marry him by pushing a glass of wine in her direction. If she drank, they became betrothed. Betrothal carried a stronger meaning than our modern concept of engagement. A betrothed woman was a married woman who had yet to consummate the marriage with her husband. She was married, however, in every other respect. An engaged woman is not married.

When Yeshua turns the water into wine at the wedding at Cana, He reveals Himself as

Yeshua fills our cup with Himself.

the Bridegroom. Yeshua's first act of ministry at a wedding starts the clock ticking towards the last wedding, the marriage supper of the Lamb. It was always a love story, even from the beginning. Recall that there are six large jars of water. This water is stored for ritual cleansing purposes. The number six represents man. In this case, it represents man's attempt to cleanse himself, and his complete inability to do so without supernatural help. Yeshua cleans us up inside and out by the wine that represents His shed blood. We enter communion by the wine and receive remission of our sins by His blood. He is the ultimate Bridegroom. He gives us everything to prepare properly for the wedding.

The Shabbat blessing over the bread is one of gratitude.

Baruch Atah Adonai, Eloheinu Melech haolam,
Ha motzi lechem min haaretz
Blessed are You, Lord our God, King of the universe,
Who brings forth bread from the earth.

The word *challah* first appears in Leviticus 24:5 to describe the twelve showbreads (*lechem hapanim*) that are arranged on the altar of the tabernacle in the wilderness. The loaves are laid out in two rows of six. The twelve represent the tribes. This provides another picture for us of the larger nation, the body of Messiah, working together in unity.

The Scriptures mandated that when the children of Israel were wandering, they were to collect just enough *manna* (a Hebrew word meaning, "What is this?") for one day's provision. The exception was on *erev Shabbat* (Sabbath evening), when they gathered twice as much to avoid working on the Sabbath. This foreshadows the double-portion blessing that Yeshua gives when we open our hearts and step into His eternal Sabbath rest.

The *challah* loaf is usually braided. It is a beautiful illustration of how God winds us together with Him in the center—a stunning picture of marriage and community in God. So many symbols, so much history! Bread is our source of life. Yeshua: the ultimate Bread of Salvation, broken and distributed to His followers, provides hope and resources for the journey.

Shabbat in the Community Called Marriage

On a practical level, how does Sabbath observance draw us as couples into communion with God and our spouses? First, the Sabbath is a time for prayer, worship, and Bible study (Acts 13:44, 16:13; Hebrews 10:24–25). These spiritual disciplines sanctify us and bring us into His presence, the place of rest. In short, the Sabbath is the one day of the week devoted to the Lord, free from the debilitating distractions that pull us apart from each other and away from the Lord.

Katharine's Perspective:
Seeing One Another Through the Blood

We can enter into Sabbath rest anytime. Yeshua is the Lord of the Sabbath. When Myles and I are in the middle of a conflict or a stressful situation, I often suggest we pause and share communion. Lo and behold, when we take the bread and the wine seriously, we tangibly feel the presence of God restore peace to our situation. David writes in Psalm 116:13 that *"I will take up the cup of salvation, and call upon the name of the LORD."* If it is good enough for David, it is good enough for me.

Every time we share the cup of wine and the bread, Myles and I remember to look at one another through the blood covering of the Lamb. We don't forget to enjoy our life together. We recall that Yeshua's first miracle was at a wedding.

Let's reflect on the word *communion*. We were meant to share life together, or to commune with one another. You are intended to commune with your spouse, your family, and with God every day, and are meant never to depart from the Sabbath rest of God. For many of us, this is difficult to accomplish. Drawing some strong boundaries with your job, your co-workers, and technology may be required. Learning how to rest and refocus on what matters most in your relationship with God and your spouse are necessary priorities.

Not entering into Sabbath rest has dire consequences. Pastor Doug Batchelor observes:

A Cornell University study confirms the detrimental effects that work-related stress can have on families. Married couples with children and burdened by long hours of work report the lowest quality of life among couples. Additionally, 43 percent of all adults suffer adverse health effects from stress, and at least 75 percent of all physician office visits are attributed to stress-related ailments, according to the American Psychological Association. Stress is also linked to the six leading causes of death in the United States: heart disease, cancer, lung ailments, accidents, cirrhosis, and suicide.[56]

God designed us to live in rest. Because of His sacrifice, we are to live in a place of Sabbath, with each other and with Him, 24/7. We are to enter into real community and social, emotional, and spiritual health. We all need to lay hold of the benefits of Yeshua's sacrifice and learn to commune and rest in Him.

Remember why God created Eve? Because He did not think it was good for man to be alone. God wants us to live life together, mutually comforting and supporting one another. Communing between husband and wife and the wider community of believers helps us in times of loss and creates the space for healing. The community is a powerful gift that unites us into one body. The ultimate community is one where we can be known and still loved in our weaknesses.

Within a marriage, there is a precious community that helps us see the larger picture. Recently a family member hurt me, but Katharine was there for me. She let me rant and rave, and then helped me get back to a healthy place. A spouse comforts and supports in the hard times.

The ultimate community is one where we can be known and still loved in our weaknesses.

I did not know how to receive comfort in my youth. My mother was disconnected because of her pain. My father passed away when I was nineteen years old. God brought me Katharine, who has the gift of helping me receive her comfort and the comfort of the Holy Spirit. She encouraged me to seek the healing I needed.

God's community is a safe place where you don't have to be afraid of people seeing your need for love and friendship. As Katharine says, "Trust God and love people. You don't trust people because people may fall short. But you can love them. Trust God to work all things together for good." This is what makes community work.

Through real communion with our spouse, family, and congregation, the Lord gives us gifts to utilize not only physically but spiritually as well. Here we can come alongside those who have failed, pick them up, and remind them of their destiny. On the other hand, the banana separated from the bunch gets peeled, as the old saying goes. Stay in the relationship and in communion.

Not long ago, some dear friends, deep believers who had been married for years, hit a rough patch in their relationship. The husband let an offense enter his heart and eventually, much to our horror, stepped away from the marriage. Watching this happen was very painful.

Katharine and I belonged to this couple's close community. Our role was to remind the wife who she was and what her call was, even if her husband abandoned it all. Without the community of spiritual family, isolation enables the volume of the destructive voice of the enemy to increase. We need immediate feedback from those we know and trust to keep us from wrong doctrine, intellectualizing the Gospel, or getting involved in ritual rather than His presence.

Of course, the community is not only for the difficult times. You can call on your friends and family to pray and watch the miracles together! This is one of the most enjoyable aspects of a community, to rejoice in victory together and to learn from one another. Katharine spent years in an intercessory prayer group praying for hours for God to move in various nations. Her prayer life was sharpened, which shaped her view of the world. When we received the mandate for Israel, we already had the world in our hearts, thanks in part to Katharine's intercessor community.

The power of that group helped us understand the "both/and" dichotomy that *"all Israel will be saved"* (Romans 11:26), but He also is *"not willing that any should perish but that all should come to repentance"* (2 Peter 3:9). This understanding was the fruit of being a part of a healthy community.

God blesses us in the natural realm in the community, too. I recently received a thank-you card from the pastors of the church that hosts our congregation, Beit Abba. In the card, one pastor wrote of how thankful he was for our lives, our ministry, and our marriage. It also included a gift check for our anniversary. This is a definite blessing of being in community.

Mostly, community protects us and keeps us balanced with our eye on the prize. Wise, mature believers sharpen us. Younger believers fill us with enthusiasm and need our mentoring.

Everyone wants to belong to a healthy community. The key to building a healthy community is to become the sort of person with whom you want to be in communion. Whatever you sow, you will reap. The community may look different than you expect. However, if you keep pouring out and giving and believing the best about people, you will eventually find that for which you are looking.

Try this at home:

When you are in Israeli society, keeping the Sabbath is easy. Most of the country shuts down every Friday evening. In America, it is more difficult to stop work and focus on God and your family for a solid twenty-four hours. Of course, Shabbat in Jewish culture can quickly go south as well when religious ritual sets in, when keeping the Sabbath rules becomes more important than caring for people.

We were once in Sacramento taking part in "The Call" with Lou Engle. It was Shabbat, and we did not have salt for the challah. So we got creative. We opened a can of salted peanuts and dipped our bread in the crushed-up peanuts. Our whole purpose of working together has been predicated on not being religious about ritual, but seeing the Holy Spirit work through ritual nonetheless. If we have a can of peanuts and there is nothing else available, we use the peanuts. You will not always be able to celebrate Shabbat on the day of Shabbat. Make Shabbat work for you with the Holy Spirit, and not according to tradition.

Whether you have a large gathering at your home or it is only you and your spouse, choose to remain in the supernatural rest and Shalom promised to us from God through His gift of Shabbat. Decide to see and be seen, to love and be loved, to comfort and be comforted. Do not become legalistic about keeping the Sabbath, but don't let your fear of becoming religious stop you from keeping the Sabbath either. The Sabbath is God's gift to His people: a precious gift we need to receive every week through entering into His rest, partaking of His body and blood, and remembering what God has done to make our rest possible. ❖

Chapter 14

ONE HEART, ONE HOPE, ONE FUTURE

One Heart

Our story, in a small way, contains answers for the contemporary dilemma on planet earth. The very planet seems to be careening and fragmenting with increasing speed. We all long for a unifying factor, one that will provide peace. Older people dream wistfully of a bygone time, which they imagine was easy and somehow made sense. Younger folks question everything, especially the flimsy constructs of a media-mad superficial society, and the wistful imagination of their elders. Katharine and I have found that in Yeshua, the Messiah, a strong unifying factor permeates our lives in a profound way.

In describing our zeitgeist, I often intentionally misquote Rav Shaul (the apostle Paul) with this paraphrase (my paraphrase in bold type):

But know this, that in the last days perilous times will come:
For men will be lovers of "selfies," lovers of money, boasters,
proud, blasphemers, disobedient to parents, unthankful,
unholy, unloving, unforgiving, slanderers, without self-
control, brutal, despisers of good." (2 Timothy 3:1–3)

Our image-driven society emphasizes social media and chronic production of "selfies." Victor Davis Hanson, the esteemed Hoover Institution scholar at Stanford, warns about the perils of "virtual virtue." We flaunt our alleged goodness before others, instead of actually doing the good works Yeshua exhorted us to produce. We can blithely critique each other from the "safe space" of our computer keyboards. We think we appear virtuous in relation to others' flaws. This produces an epidemic of divisive life, just as Messiah Yeshua warned:

Or how can you say to your brother, "Brother, let me
remove the speck that is in your eye," when you yourself do
not see the plank that is in your own eye? Hypocrite! First
remove the plank from your own eye, and then you will
see clearly to remove the speck that is in your brother's eye.
(Luke 6:42)

Sigmund Freud (who was wrong about many things, but understood some things) called this "projection," and it is rampant today, especially on the Internet. We *project* onto others the very feelings and struggles we have within ourselves. My greed, lust, rage, or any sin is attributed to another in an attempt to distance myself from unflattering or uncomfortable inner realities. We blithely assume that any weakness in another person is a reason to go in for the kill and tear them down with our own "virtual virtue."

We have democratized opinion to such a degree that it can pass for factual knowledge of a person or their situation. But do we really *know* them? Do we have daily interaction with them? These interpersonal gaps affect our homes.

The process of working through issues in an honest way leads us to the idea of "One Heart." This is not automatic. It does not come with the marriage license or even the most beautiful wedding ceremony. "One Heart" must be grasped and worked into our lives. By *One Heart* we mean the experience of spiritual and emotional unity. We do not mean blind conformity—there will always be differences between us. The unity of "One Heart" provides a shared experience of shalom—of peace, wholeness, and rest. Our marriage becomes an oasis of harmony when viewed against the turmoil of life.

By One Heart *we mean the experience of spiritual and emotional unity.*

Remember, we are made in the image of God. Our very nature is triune: spirit, soul, and body, like the Father, Son, and Holy Spirit. Wisdom goads us to remember the *Shema* of Deuteronomy 6:

> *"Hear, O Israel: The LORD our God, the LORD is one! You shall love the LORD your God with all your heart, with all your soul, and with all your strength. And these words which I command you today shall be in your heart. You*

shall teach them diligently to your children, and shall talk of them when you sit in your house, when you walk by the way, when you lie down, and when you rise up. You shall bind them as a sign on your hand, and they shall be as frontlets between your eyes. You shall write them on the doorposts of your house and on your gates."
(Deuteronomy 6:4–9)

In this seminal prayer, we find the hidden treasure of oneness. The Hebrew "one" in this verse is *echad*, and it is an expression of compound unity. More than the sum of its parts, it speaks of a supernatural oneness between three: Father, Son, and Holy Spirit. As a reflection of God, our marriage and family life can also reflect that oneness. With time, we begin to experience "One Heart." This is possible because of the sacrifice of Yeshua:

For He Himself is our peace, who has made both one, and has broken down the middle wall of separation, having abolished in His flesh the enmity, that is, the law of commandments contained in ordinances, so as to create in Himself one new man from the two, thus making peace, and that He might reconcile them both to God in one body through the cross, thereby putting to death the enmity. And He came and preached peace to you who were afar off and to those who were near. For through Him we both have access by one Spirit to the Father. (Ephesians 2:14–18)

One Hope

We love to bring spiritually hungry pilgrims to Greece, Turkey, and Israel. In Turkey, we often visit Ephesus and in the ruins there we teach from Paul's letter to the Ephesians. As our friends soak in the rich history of the dramatic ruins, they are also confronted with the biblical admonition and exhortation regarding the life of those outside of Messiah. The mandate on Paul required a strong sense of the Jewishness of the Gospel and a remarkable ability to translate it into the culture of the day. The idea of hope is woven throughout the Hebrew Scriptures and culminates with the Messianic promises, fulfilled by Yeshua HaMashiach. Paul wrote it this way:

The idea of hope is woven throughout the Hebrew Scriptures.

> *And you He made alive, who were dead in trespasses and sins, in which you once walked according to the course of this world, according to the prince of the power of the air, the spirit who now works in the sons of disobedience. . . . Therefore remember that you, once Gentiles in the flesh—who are called Uncircumcision by what is called the Circumcision made in the flesh by hands—that at that time you were without Christ, being aliens from the commonwealth of Israel and strangers from the covenants of promise, having no hope and without God in the world. But now in Christ Jesus you who once were far off have been brought near by the blood of Christ. . . . Now, therefore, you are no longer strangers and foreigners, but fellow citizens with the saints and members of the household of God,*

having been built on the foundation of the apostles and prophets, Jesus Christ Himself being the chief cornerstone, in whom the whole building, being fitted together, grows into a holy temple in the Lord, in whom you also are being built together for a dwelling place of God in the Spirit. (Ephesians 2:1–2, 11–13, 19–22)

Where is hope? In whom is hope? In the promised Messiah of Israel, the One prophesied in Genesis 3:15. Speaking to the enemy of our souls, God proclaims the coming of Messiah:

"And I will put enmity between you and the woman, and between your seed and her Seed; He shall bruise your head, and you shall bruise His heel."

It would cost the Redeemer dearly, but the adversary would be crushed by His finished work. The one hope for the inhabitants of planet earth is the Messiah of Israel and Savior of the world. It is so right that the modern-day Israeli national anthem in the Hebrew language is called "HaTikvah," meaning "The Hope."

We were in China working with the underground church leaders. During a break from our teaching, we visited the Shanghai Israeli Refugees Museum. This wonder is a monument to the Jewish exiles from Europe who found a safe haven in Shanghai during the twentieth-century Nazi era. The Chinese preserved their lives and the Jewish people were able to preserve their religion and culture. Our hosts had never seen it, but they exclaimed, "No wonder Shanghai is the financial capital of China. We honored the mandate of Genesis 12:1–3!"

Now the LORD had said to Abram: "Get out of your country, from your family and from your father's house, to a land that I will show you. I will make you a great nation; I will bless you and make your name great; and you shall be a blessing. I will bless those who bless you, and I will curse him who curses you; and in you all the families of the earth shall be blessed."

As we stood in the balcony of the museum's synagogue, an Israeli tour group arrived below us. I heard Hebrew being spoken, but I thought, *"Hebrew? In China? No way!"* I was flabbergasted as they lined up before the bema (altar) and sang "HaTikvah"! We exchanged pleasantries in a mix of Hebrew and English. I prayed silently for their eyes to open to the ultimate meaning of HaTikvah: The Hope of Israel, Messiah Yeshua.

The book of Matthew begins, *"The book of the genealogy of Jesus Christ, the Son of David, the Son of Abraham: Abraham begot Isaac, Isaac begot Jacob, and Jacob begot Judah and his brothers. . . . Boaz begot Obed by Ruth, Obed begot Jesse, and Jesse begot David the king. . . . Jacob begot Joseph the husband of Mary, of whom was born Jesus who is called Christ"* (Matthew 1:1-2, 5-6, 16). Yeshua was born to a specific family due to a promise made by a covenant-keeping God. For Katharine and me, He is our One Hope.

One Future

Our world is full of seekers wondering about the meaning of life and their place in the universe. All our collective seeking is really a quest for love. Many of us spend years "looking for love in all the wrong places," to quote an old country song. Even when we find the human love of our life, we need to work through disappointments and ongoing differences. Is there no perfect one for us? Will we ever meet our soul mate? We are convinced that if we ever did, life would be smooth sailing under the glow of a perfect pink sunset. Here's good news and bad news:

First, the bad news

Even the best marriages face trauma, trouble, and trials! We know this through experience, and have ministered to many solid couples—people of faith—that weathered tough times together. That's because not one of us is perfect.

Now the good news

There is a Bridegroom of Heaven who is perfect. Whether you are male or female, He is the Prince of the old song, "Someday my prince will come." His desire for you is so great that He came from heaven to be the divine sacrificial Lamb pictured in the Hebrew Scriptures. That sacrifice opens the door for an eternal relationship with the God of Abraham through a marriage to Yeshua. Although He came as a lamb, He is returning to rule and reign as the Lion of Judah. His victory celebration will last a thousand years and as His Bride, we will be at His right hand throughout that era.

So, let me exhort you, as your Rabbi/Pastor/Doc, alongside my faithful bride: would you invite Him into your life?

Just admit you are imperfect and need the Messiah, the Holy

One of Israel.

For all have sinned and fall short of the glory of God. (Romans 3:23)

That's me!

For the wages of sin is death, but the gift of God is eternal life in Christ Jesus our Lord. (Romans 6:23)

That's the gift I need!

But He was wounded for our transgressions, He was bruised for our iniquities; the chastisement for our peace was upon Him, and by His stripes we are healed. (Isaiah 53:5)

But God demonstrates His own love toward us, in that while we were still sinners, Christ died for us. (Romans 5:8)

That's what I want!

If you confess with your mouth the Lord Jesus and believe in your heart that God has raised Him from the dead, you will be saved. (Romans 10:9)

But as many as received Him, to them He gave the right to become children of God, to those who believe in His name. (John 1:12)

You may be thinking, "That does describe me, it is what I need and want, but it can't be that simple! You mean to say that even if I don't currently believe, I can ask *heaven for the faith* to believe in Yeshua? After all my striving and religious activity and good works (or evil deeds), you are saying that I can start fresh in this life, with a promise of eternity with the One Who Is Love?"

Yes, that is what we are saying! Try this and find out what happens as you *Marry Up* with the Bridegroom of Heaven! ❖

Notes

[1]Albert Einstein, "What Life Means to Einstein: An Interview by George Sylvester Viereck," *The Saturday Evening Post*, Oct. 26, 1929, 17.

[2]Moishe Rosen, *Y'Shua: The Jewish Way to Say Jesus* (Chicago: Moody, 1982).

[3]Stan Telchin, *Betrayed!* (Grand Rapids: Chosen Books, 1981).

[4]Ceil and Moishe Rosen, *Christ in the Passover* (Chicago: Moody, 1978).

[5]Tara Parker-Pope, "Is Marriage Good for Your Health?" *The New York Times Magazine*, April 14, 2010, http://www.nytimes.com/2010/04/18/magazine/18marriage-t.html?_r=0.

[6]Lecia Bushak, "Married Vs Single: What Science Says Is Better For Your Health," *Medical Daily*, April 2, 2015, http://www.medicaldaily.com/married-vs-single-what-science-says-better-your-health-327878.

[7]Parker-Pope, "Is Marriage Good for Your Health?"

[8]"Issues in Jewish Ethics: Marriage," *Jewish Virtual Library*, from Avi Hein, Sarah Szymkowicz, and Brigitte Dayan, "Pearls, henna and challah: Sephardic nuptial customs," *Jewish News Weekly of Northern California*, November 8, 1996, https://www.jewishvirtuallibrary.org/jsource/Judaism/marriage.html.

[9]See Genesis 2:21–25. Any other creative pairing humans come up with, whether homosexuality, sex outside of marriage, or polyamory, leads to death. But you don't have to rely on Scripture alone to discern what nature makes evident; maximum health, pleasure, and the future of the human race (the ability to procreate without the help of scientific intervention) all affirm that marriage between one man and one woman for life is the best way to go.

[10]Glenn Kay, "Jewish Wedding Customs and the Bride of Messiah," *Grafted-In Ministries*, http://messianicfellowship.50webs.com/wedding.html.

[11]Ibid.

[12]Ibid.

[13]Asher Intrater, "Power Of The Blood," Revive Israel Ministries, *Searching His Ways*, September 19, 2010, http://searchinghisways.blogspot.com/2010/09/power-of-blood-asher-intrater.html.

[14]Asher Intrater, "Yeshua Not Only Bled, But Poured Out His Soul," *Charisma News*, March 29, 2013, http://www.charismanews.com/opinion/38853-yeshua-

not-only-bled-but-poured-out-his-soul.

[15]Kay, "Jewish Wedding Customs."

[16]Ibid.

[17]Ibid.

[18]Intrater, "A People Made Ready," Revive Israel, *Tikkun International*, https://www.tikkunministries.org/newsletters/ai-sep05.php.

[19]Jerry Bock and Sheldon Harnick, "Do You Love Me?" 1964, from *Fiddler on the Roof*.

[20]Michael Youssef, "Ordinary People, Extraordinary Prayers," July 3, 2016, http://www.ltw.org/listen/teaching/series/ordinary-people-extraordinary-prayers/part-1.

[21]Lennon-McCartney, "The End," 1969, from *Abbey Road*, Apple Records, London.

[22]Quote from *Rocky*, 1976, John G. Avildsen, dir., United Artists.

[23]"Issues in Jewish Ethics: 'Kosher' Sex," *Jewish Virtual Library*, http://www.jewishvirtuallibrary.org/quot-kosher-quot-sex.

[24]Quote from *As Good As It Gets*, 1997, James L. Brooks, dir., TriStar Pictures.

[25]Emerson Eggerichs, "Believing the Best About Your Spouse," *Focus on the Family*, 2011, http://www.thrivingfamily.com/Features/Magazine/2011/believing-the-best-about-your-spouse.aspx.

[26]Gary Chapman, *The 5 Love Languages: The Secret to Love That Lasts* (Nashville: Lifeway Press, 2007).

[27]"Mark Twain Quotes," http://www.brainyquote.com/quotes/quotes/m/marktwain100358.html.

[28]Havilah Cunnington, *The Naked Truth About Sexuality* (Redding, CA: Create Space Publishing, 2015), 82.

[29]Ibid., 82–86.

[30]Asher Intrater, "Faithful Friend," *Ministries of Francis Frangipane*, 2011, http://francisfrangipanemessages.blogspot.com/2011/06/faithful-friend-by-asher-intrater.html..

[31]Youssef, "Ordinary People."

[32]Barry and Lori Byrne, *Love After Marriage* (Ventura CA: Regal Books, 2012), 33.

[33]Tzipporah Price, "Marriage: A Relationship Between Real People," *Chabad. org* blog *Can This Marriage Be Saved?*, July 2, 2010, http://www.chabad.org/ blogs/blog_cdo/aid/1230849/jewish/Marriage-A-Relationship-Between- Real-People.htm.

[34]Ibid.

[35]Yanki Tauber, "Bless You!" *Chabad.org*, http://www.chabad.org/library/ article_cdo/aid/3072/jewish/Bless-You.htm.

[36]Dr. Caroline Leaf, "His Brain—Her Brain, Session 1," February 12, 2016, http://coastalchurch.org/message-archive/dr-caroline-leaf/session-1/.

[37]Sara Esther Crispe, "Words That Hurt, Words That Heal," *Chabad.org* blog *Musing for Meaning*, April 9, 2012, http://www.chabad.org/blogs/blog_cdo/ aid/1808170/jewish/Words-That-Hurt-Words-That-Heal.htm.

[38]Ibid.

[39]Jack Zenger and Joseph Folkman, "The Ideal Praise-to-Criticism Ratio," *Harvard Business Review*, March 15, 2015, https://hbr.org/2013/03/the-ideal- praise-to-criticism.

[40]Rabbi Jonathan Sacks, "How to Praise," *Chabad.org*, http://www.chabad. org/parshah/article_cdo/aid/2504368/jewish/How-to-Praise.htm.

[41]Ibid.

[42]Tori deAngelis, "When anger's a plus," *American Psychological Association*, March, 2003, http://www.apa.org/monitor/mar03/whenanger.aspx.

[43]Rebetzin Tziporah Heller, "Men & Women: Jewish View of Gender Differences," *Aish.com*, http://www.aish.com/ci/w/48955181.html.

[44]Ibid.

[45]Dr. Caroline Leaf, "His Brain—Her Brain, Session 2," February 13, 2016, http://coastalchurch.org/message-archive/dr-caroline-leaf/brain-brain- session-2/.

[46]Leaf, "His Brain—Her Brain, Session 1."

[47]Dr. Caroline Leaf, "His Brain—Her Brain, Session 3," 2016, https://vimeo. com/155856231/.

[48]Mark Gungor, "Men's Brains and Women's Brains with Mark Gungor (Nothing Box)," https://www.youtube.com/watch?v=SZ6mVumHY9I.

[49]Leaf, "His Brain—Her Brain, Session 1."

[50]Ibid.

⁵¹Ibid.

⁵²Ibid.

⁵³Billy Crystal, *700 Sundays* (New York: Grand Central Publishing, 2005).

⁵⁴Shlomo Shulman, "The Sabbath as a Bride," *Jewish Answers.org*, http://www.jewishanswers.org/ask-the-rabbi-date/2011/03/?p=2913.

⁵⁵Simi Lichtman, "Just Married," *The Forward*, May 9, 2013, http://forward.com/just-married/176248/shabbat-the-marriage-cure/.

⁵⁶Pastor Doug Batchelor, "Seize the Day: Keeping the Sabbath Holy—Part 2," *Amazing Facts*, July 15, 2013, http://www.amazingfacts.org/news-and-features/inside-report/magazine/id/10802/t/seize-the-day-keeping-the-sabbath-holypart-2.